HAZARD MITIGATION TRAINING FOR VULNERABLE COMMUNITIES

This book is designed to educate vulnerable communities, emergency practitioners, and disaster researchers to increase the social and physical capacity of communities to mitigate and adapt to disaster impacts. With climate change escalating the intensity and range of disasters, we have entered an unprecedented time. The tools in this book allow researchers, practitioners, and community leaders to adopt new training techniques that are more engaging and effective, using a bottom-up framework to integrate knowledge, attitude, preparedness, and skills (K.A.P.S).

This book is uniquely designed to support instructors, researchers, practitioners, and community leaders in their effort to promote preparedness across marginalized communities. The book contains a full range of templates, worksheets, survey questions, background information, and guidance for carrying out training; the material has been field-validated to meet research standards.

The K.A.P.S. Framework outlined throughout the book is designed to serve as an adaptable model that national and international audiences can utilize to better prepare their communities for disasters due to hurricanes, floods, and tornadoes. As climate change continues to ravage communities, the K.A.P.S. training program will prove to be an important tool for community trainers and academics across a range of hazards and disasters.

Joy Semien is an interdisciplinary multi-hazard research scientist and community capacity builder. She holds a BSc in Biology from Dillard University and a MSc in Urban Planning and Environmental Policy from Texas Southern University, where she created the K.A.P.S. Framework to train high-risk communities. Joy works as a research assistant for the Hazard Reduction and Recovery Center at Texas A&M University where she is completing her doctoral degree in Urban and Regional Sciences. She has centered her doctoral research on examining the immediate impact and short-term recovery of small businesses and nonprofits that have experienced compounded events.

Joy's research interest focuses on developing methods to uniquely bridge systemic gaps across disciplines while exploring the intersectionality of hazards, race, and social justice. Ultimately, she seeks to turn research into action to increase marginalized, multi-hazard communities' ability to prepare, respond, and recover from disasters.

Earthea Nance is committed to working with vulnerable communities at disproportionate risk of disasters, pollution, and inadequate infrastructure. In December 2021, she was appointed by President Biden to serve as the Regional Administrator for the Environmental Protection Agency, Region 6. Dr. Nance previously served as a public official for the City of New Orleans after Hurricane Katrina, where she managed $60 million in flood mitigation funds and established the city's first approved plans for hazard mitigation, sustainability, and green energy. As a scholar, Earthea developed and implemented disaster training programs and conducted community-based research on the impacts of major disasters in Gulf Coast communities and in communities without access to water and sanitation in Brazil and Mozambique. As an advocate, she brought community and equity perspectives into regional disaster policy in the Houston metro area. Earthea earned a PhD in Civil and Environmental Engineering from Stanford University, and MSc and BSc degrees from the University of California-Davis. She previously taught at Texas Southern University, the University of New Orleans, Massachusetts Institute of Technology, and Virginia Tech.

Disaster Risk Reduction and Resilience Series

The Disaster Risk Reduction and Resilience series serves the international urban and regional planning community, as well as those in related disciplines including public administration, architecture, engineering, political science, sociology, environmental and physical sciences, and the many disciplines connected to disaster work and research. The series brings together a cross-disciplinary group of experienced researchers and practitioners to author timely, inter-disciplinary and practical information for practitioners, students and researchers.

Hazard Mitigation Training for Vulnerable Communities

A K.A.P.S. (Knowledge, Attitude, Preparedness, Skills) Approach

Joy Semien and Earthea Nance

Routledge
Taylor & Francis Group

NEW YORK AND LONDON

Cover Image: Joy Semien

First published 2022
by Routledge
605 Third Avenue, New York, NY 10158

and by Routledge
4 Park Square, Milton Park, Abingdon, Oxon, OX14 4RN

Routledge is an imprint of the Taylor & Francis Group, an informa business

Library of Congress Cataloguing-in-Publication Data
Names: Semien, Joy, author. | Nance, Earthea, 1962- author.
Title: Hazard mitigation training for vulnerable communities: a K.A.P.S. (knowledge, attitude, preparedness, skills) approach / Joy Semien and Earthea Nance.
Description: New York, NY: Routledge, 2022. | Includes bibliographical references and index. |
Identifiers: LCCN 2021052689 (print) | LCCN 2021052690 (ebook) | ISBN 9781032010717 (hardback) | ISBN 9781032010700 (paperback) | ISBN 9781003177005 (ebook)
Subjects: LCSH: Hazard mitigation. | Emergency management.
Classification: LCC HV551.2 .S45 2022 (print) | LCC HV551.2 (ebook) | DDC 363.34/8--dc23/eng/20211105
LC record available at https://lccn.loc.gov/2021052689
LC ebook record available at https://lccn.loc.gov/2021052690

ISBN: 978-1-032-01071-7 (hbk)
ISBN: 978-1-032-01070-0 (pbk)
ISBN: 978-1-003-17700-5 (ebk)

DOI: 10.4324/9781003177005

Typeset in Sabon
by MPS Limited, Dehradun

We dedicate this book to the many community leaders of marginalized communities who continue to fight to ensure that future generations will live a long and healthy life.

We also dedicate this book to the community leaders who have passed on, leaving the torch to the next generation of climate and environmental justice leaders.

This book is also dedicated to Mr. Amos Favorite and Dr. William Anderson whose life works are highlighted in the K.A.P.S. legacy spotlights after Part I and Part III of this book.

While not featured in the book, we dedicate this book to Mr. Richard Brown, Mr. Edward Jackson, Ms. Nita Jackson, and the many other community leaders who fearlessly advocated for environmental justice for the Geismar, Louisiana community.

Finally, we dedicate this book to marginalized communities across the United States and the world. We recognize that marginalization is a global issue that we hope this book helps bring to an end.

Contents

Illustrations

Boxes

Contributors

Alessandra Jerolleman, Ph.D., Alessandra Jerolleman, LLC

Bakeyah Nelson, Ph.D., Climate Imperative and Community Health Collaborative Consulting

Bridgette Murray, R.N., Achieving Community Tasks Successfully (ACTS)

David Padgett, Ph.D., Geomental Consulting

Jamila Johnson, P.E., C.F.M., Walter P. Moore

Kathe Hambrick, River Road African American Museum

Lori Peek, Ph.D., Natural Hazards Center, University of Colorado Boulder

Maliaka Favorite, M.F.A, Artist and Environmental Advocate

Michelle Meyer, Ph.D., Hazard Reduction and Recovery Center, Texas A&M University

Monique Harden, Esq., Deep South Center for Environmental Justice

Nathanael Stephens, Chief Firefighter Geismar, Louisiana

Norma Anderson, William Averette Anderson Fund

Pamela Hernandez, Ph.D., Educo Research

Quianta Moore, M.D., Ph.D., Catapult Dreams LLC

Sharon Lavigne, RISE St. James

Tamu Favorite, B.A., Actor, Writer, and Environmental Advocate

Foreword

Communities across the world are grappling with a quickly changing environment that brings more frequent and intense disaster losses. While climate change is spreading these impacts to areas often unaffected, communities of color, low-income communities, and populations that are stigmatized and marginalized in society have always faced higher risks of disaster impacts and longer recovery timelines. The past few decades have seen increasing scholarly interest and focus on these disparities in policies, laws, and practices that generate unequal outcomes across various social characteristics. Yet, while research accumulates, the "boots on the ground" work in and with communities to create change still remains. This handbook helps close that gap between knowledge and practice – and makes all communities more resilient to hazards today and tomorrow.

The authors of *Hazard Mitigation Training for Vulnerable Communities: A K.A.P.S. (Knowledge, Attitude, Preparedness, Skills) Approach* present a unique model to help convert research into action. The authors begin the handbook by first offering a brief literature review of topics important to understand why we need equitable and adaptable approaches that meet communities where they are. These topics include disaster education, climate resilience and justice, and the social construction of disaster vulnerability. Next, the authors unpack the "K.A.P.S. Model" using both theory and practice by explaining the importance of applying Knowledge, Attitude, Preparedness, and Skills to disaster resilience education. Throughout Chapters 4 and 5 the authors provide example lesson plans that can be used to teach the concepts with communities. Finally, the authors illustrate how to implement and evaluate a K.A.P.S. Community Training Course from start to finish.

The K.A.P.S. Model is transformative as it uses a bottom-up methodology to first obtain demographic information on the community prior to beginning. This information helps to guide the authors and the users of the Model about what concepts and the level of details that need to be presented to ensure comprehension, translation, interpretation, and extrapolation. In addition, this information helps instructors decide which analogies should or should not be used during the presentation to avoid various biases that can complicate the learning process. The K.A.P.S. Model focuses on the importance of building trust and relationships through genuine engagement prior to any trainings, and accounts for the various needs of participants to increase engagement such as providing meals, snacks, child-care, and take-home material. The K.A.P.S. Model aims to build instructors who are reachable and accessible not just for the one-time workshop but as a symbol of the long-term commitment to the community.

A handbook like this offers a bridge for researchers, practitioners, and community leaders to uniquely engage with residents to ensure that they are wearing their *Disaster K.A.P.S.* prior to the onset of a disaster.

Michelle Annette Meyer, Ph.D.,
Director of the Hazard Reduction and
Recovery Center at Texas A&M University

Preface

The purpose of this handbook is to provide practitioners, researchers, and community leaders with a brief guide on ways to increase the capacity of community members to prepare for hazard events. The handbook uses the Knowledge, Attitude, Preparedness, and Skills (K.A.P.S.) Model to guide the work with multi-hazard communities of color and/or low-income communities. These are the communities most often at risk and most able to benefit from K.A.P.S. training. Our main goal through this work is to encourage those who are working with vulnerable communities to embody a bottom-up approach as compared to the typical top-down approach. The bottom-up approach is centered around understanding the community, building awareness, soliciting participation, and encouraging engagement. We recognize that K.A.P.S. is only one model that can be used to guide practitioners, researchers and community leaders to prepare for hazard events. Based on the findings of our research it is our belief that this tool can serve as a model to reduce fatalities, injuries, and economic losses among multi-hazard communities of low income and/or color.

HANDBOOK COMPONENTS

This handbook fills a gap in what is currently available on the topic of disaster education. While existing books are oriented to the needs of emergency practitioners and disaster researchers, this book is designed to support community leaders in addition to practitioners and researchers. The tools in this book allow community leaders, researchers, and practitioners, to adopt a bottom-up approach to developing training techniques that are engaging and effective. These techniques are derived from the findings of education research and from the fieldwork of Semien (2019), Nance (2004), and others. The book is unique because it is comprised of instructional worksheets, handouts, best practices, community activist spotlights, and practitioner spotlights.

The book is divided into three parts. Part I of this handbook introduces the reader to the concepts of the disaster cycle, impacts of the cycle on communities of color, bottom-up methods to increasing community capacity, climate resilience and justice, and the social constructs associated with vulnerable communities. Part II of this handbook introduces the K.A.P.S. Model and provides a basic framework for applying knowledge, attitude, preparedness, and skills when working with multi-hazardous communities of color and/or those of low income. Part III provides a case study example from Geismar, Louisiana where the K.A.P.S. Model was first implemented. This section also provides a method of measurement and a list of national as well as international resources that may be helpful for working with multi-hazard and marginalized communities.

Acknowledgements

We are grateful to the contributors of this handbook whose stories help offer a greater level of insight to the work of climate and environmental justice. We recognize that we are only pieces of a larger puzzle but hope that this one piece can add value for generations to come.

We would also like to say thank you to Yujie Wang, Chandler Wilkins, Allen White, Eritrea Jean-Felix, Ashley Helms, Lekita Page, Destiny Ward, Faith Ward, Lynette Ward, Joseph Allen, Precious Mitchell, Sharon Semien, Sedonia Ward, Lisa Delafance whose support aided in the completion of this book. Without their help this book would have been a challenge to complete.

Abbreviations

ABC Model	Antecedents, Behavior, Consequences
BCA	Benefit-cost analysis
BIPOC	Black, Indigenous, People of Color
CAB	Community Advisory Board
CERT	Community Emergency Response Team
CDC	Center for Disease Control
COVID-19	COVID-19 Novel Coronavirus discovered in 2019
DSCEJ	Deep South Center for Environmental Justice
DMV	Department of Motor Vehicles
ESRI	Environmental Systems Research Institute, Inc.
FEMA	Federal Emergency Management Agency
FMA	Flood Mitigation Assistance
GIS	Geographic Information System
HMGP	Hazard Mitigation Grant Program
K.A.P.S.	Knowledge, Attitude, Preparedness, and Skills
LMI	Low-to-moderate income
myRTK	My Right to Know Application
RL	Repetitive Loss
RSEI	Risk Screening Environmental Indicators
SRL	Severe Repetitive Loss
TRI	Toxic Release Inventory
VARK Model	Visual, Aural, Read/write, and Kinesthetic sensory modalities
UNHCR	United Nations High Commissioner for Refugees

PART I

Disasters and Communities

···

The study of hazards and disasters is a relatively new field of research but a necessary one as disasters are increasing in intensity and frequency. In its early years, it was assumed that disasters were just an anomaly, creating random losses across entire communities (Scandlyn et al., 2013; Anderson, 1965). However, in recent decades researchers have challenged this assumption, making it clear that disasters are often the result of "social processes of marginalization that produce unequal risks to hazards" (Bolin et al., 1998: 96). These unequal risks to hazards are often the result of (1) historical discrimination and (2) the inability of a community to account for the vast diversity of social characteristics within a community.

According to the theory of social vulnerability, disparities within a community are often the result of social structures such as through racially or economically biased laws and procedures (Morrow, 1999; Bullard and Wright, 2008). This in part is due to patterns of historically discriminatory land-use policies like that of redlining and racial discrimination which marginalized individuals and limited their access to safer geographical areas (Yinger, 1991; Gilmore, 2002; Enarson and Fordham, 2000). Many hazard researchers have used the theory of social vulnerability to indicate that disasters often place small communities, especially those of color and/or of low income, at a disproportionately high risk for disaster occurrence (Thomas et al., 2013). These inequities often leave marginalized groups with a limited ability to recover their household after a disaster (Highfield et al., 2014; Bolin and Kurtz, 2017). As a result, these patterns of marginalization increase the susceptibility of individuals, families, and businesses to disasters. When social characteristics, like those described above, are not considered throughout the disaster planning cycle, it creates pockets of disproportionality that increase the vulnerability of these groups.

Throughout this first section of the handbook, we seek to examine the impacts of disproportionality among vulnerable multi-hazard communities through the lens of

DOI: 10.4324/9781003177005-1

climate resilience and justice while presenting a series of best practices that can be used when working with these communities. Understanding how communities respond to various hazards can help practitioners, researchers, and community leaders develop appropriate processes to help communities reduce their risk of loss of life and property (Brooks, 2002; Allmendinger, 2009; Corburn, 2003).

BOX P.1 K.A.P.S. LEGACY SPOTLIGHT 1

Dr. William Averette and Mrs. Norma Anderson
Founder, WIlliam Averette Anderson Fund

Q1. Your husband was an integral part of inspiring individuals from marginalized groups to pursue a career in disaster research. Why do you think it was important for him to take up this journey?

I think initially given his personal background, of having grown up in a marginalized community and raised by this grandparents, it really inspired him to think beyond where he was. He also had mentors that introduced him to the field of hazards and disasters, where Bill very quickly realized that there was an exclusion of the needs and the interest of individuals of marginalized groups. So not only from his personal background, having been reared in Akron, AL, and seeing some of the impacts of environment there, but not realizing it then. As he trained and went to graduate school, he realized that the thing [poverty] that they experienced growing up, not everyone was experiencing. He realized there were things that could have been and still needed to be done. Bill realized that having had that experience was beneficial, many people, most people in the field, at that time did not come to it with that same knowledge and reasoning. I think that's why his work was so important to him.

Q2. What is the significance of the legacy he has left behind?

Bill was a trailblazer in earthquake engineering, although he was a sociologist. He helped to spearhead the development of the National Center for Earthquake Engineering Research at the National Science Foundation. In terms of trailblazing as an African American, he set the stage for this, he was willing to think and produce research that was off the cuff. The unachievable is the key to any black and brown person's achievements as trailblazers. I think, he also realized the significance of being in the room where decisions were being made. As a minority, sometimes you have to prove that you are worthy to be in the room, even though you know that you may be more than worthy. His legacy is why I developed the Bill Anderson Fund because it is important for young scholars of color to be in the room, where the research and decisions are happening. The Fund provides a network for marginalized students who are now part of Bill's legacy.

Q3. Now you are an integral part of inspiring individuals from marginalized groups to pursue a career in disaster research, why is this work so important for you to continue?

I realized that Bill, an African American, was one of very few who looked like him that could help push the concepts forward of needing to have the representation of marginalized groups in the work that involved them and their communities. That was the reason I spearheaded the development of the Bill Anderson Fund and that's where we are today. We are interviewing 23 new applicants, we have 34 current fellows, and 26 alumni. The ultimate goal is to have 100 in 10 years. Now who could have imagined that! In being a trailblazer, you have to know that it can be done and have the willingness to create something. You have to also have the support from a number of people to help make it happen and you have to trust them that they will be able to help you be successful with carrying out the dream.

Q5. What do you hope your legacy will be after you have passed on?

I hope my legacy will be that of the Bill Anderson Fund which is something that I could never have imagined, but I never had a doubt that it could be achieved. Unfortunately, its development happened because my husband died. I don't know if that had not happened the Fund would exist. So out of something horrific for me, it allowed the growth of something spectacular. I would imagine that my legacy would be being able to set my grief aside and draw energy and strength from the relationship that I had with my husband for 45 years of marriage and be able to envision something that he would have been tremendously proud of and wanted to create, which also embodies the legacy of my family: education.

Q6. If you had to give advice for someone who is aspiring to have such a profound career as a disaster researcher what would that advice be?

- Never be discouraged because you know your life is never on a positive path. Always, you'll have struggles. You'll have challenges. You'll have some failures, but keep your eyes on the prize—keep pushing forward.
- Do not allow someone to tell you that you cannot do something. Take those kinds of words and allow them to be an inspiration for you to have an opportunity to shine.
- Don't fear asking for help.
- Be a willing partner with other people who need help. So, you can be a part of their success and they can be a part of yours.
- Be as positive as possible. Do not take defeat as a personal indication of your inability because there are going to be defeats.

Learn more about Dr. William "Bill" and Norma Anderson: https://billandersonfund.org/

CHAPTER 1

Disaster Education as a Form of Community Capacity Building

In recent years both government and non-governmental entities have made it a point to educate vulnerable communities, those most at risk, on the importance of disaster preparedness. These large entities provide both online resources as well as occasional community workshops that address key disaster concerns (Wingate et al., 2007; Sutton and Tierney, 2006). However, one of the biggest problems with these resources is that they use a top-down approach to train and/or communicate with these communities. This is problematic because communities' voices and experiences go unheeded (Anguiano et al., 2012; Hofrichter, 1993). This chapter will compare top-down versus bottom-up approaches to working with marginalized communities.

TOP-DOWN

The top-down approach can be defined as "the concern of ruling groups to incorporate and integrate subordinate groups into the dominant ideology in order to ensure their own security and sustainability" (Popple and Quinney, 2002: 72). In other words, it is the ability of larger groups like hazard researchers, professionals, and governmental officials to enter a community and provide vast knowledge in a manner that may not be received by the target community. As a result, the top-down information and resources provided by big entities may go unheeded (Enenkel et al., 2017; Baudoin et al., 2016; Pandey and Okazaki, 2005). This is often because the facilitator enters the community with the cognitive perception that the information provided is the only method to effectively proceed through the entire disaster cycle. The failure of the facilitator in this case is that they do not account for the community's capacity to adapt prior to the suggested behavioral changes introduced by the entities (Gundlach and McDonough, 2011). In some cases, residents living in multi-hazard socially vulnerable communities may develop adaptive behavior to

DOI: 10.4324/9781003177005-2

reduce their risk of loss of life and property (Olsson and Folke, 2001; Suda, 2000). Through adaptive behavior residents take steps to develop strategies to cope with climatic uncertainties (Adger and Vincent, 2005; Olsson and Folke, 2001; Suda, 2000).

Another problem with the top-down approach is that the facilitator often fails to provide information that is socially and culturally relatable to multi-hazard communities of color and/or of low income (Paris and Alim, 2017). This is problematic because if an individual in a community can understand neither the verbal nor written commands by the entity then the information is not valuable. Language can be the very thing that both connects and disconnects people from the social structures that exist within a society (Wallace and Wolf, 2006). This disconnect is often the result of poor communication among various social groups and/or organizations (Brooks, 2002; Allmendinger, 2009). Poor communication can lead to unheeded information, increasing communities' susceptibility to disaster and increasing the risk for loss of life and property. Another aspect of this is when the facilitator is unaware of how social systems, economic systems and policies directly or indirectly cause harm to vulnerable groups and ignore their needs.

BOTTOM-UP

The key to successfully approaching a multi-hazard community of color and/or low income is not through a top-down approach but through a bottom-up approach. A bottom-up approach can be defined as a "community-driven approach in promoting community participation and building local capacity within the social, institutional and political context" (Babajanian, 2009: 449). In other words, incorporating key community stakeholders into the planning process, prior to delivering trainings, materials, or other deliverables to the community. This will ensure that the training and other informationals are socially and culturally appropriate. To effectively engage with the community, we must understand the choices people make based on their overall present-day experiences (Allmendinger, 2009; Wallace and Wolf, 2006). In a sense, before an entity even steps foot into a community they should seek to understand the community's level of conscientiousness that reveals "what it would be like in someone else's skin" (Wallace and Wolf, 2006: 180). A bottom-up approach creates the context for inclusion. The reality is that communities are made of highly complex social systems that are constantly evolving to seek true change. Community leaders, at the least, should be actively involved (Brooks, 2002; Wallace and Wolf, 2006; Allmendinger, 2009).

One benefit of approaching local communities with a bottom-up approach is that it allows the facilitator to gain entrance into the community while building trust and gaining general knowledge (Gundlach and McDonough, 2011). Generally, community leaders have a greater bond with local community members, based on trust (Christopher et al., 2008; Bos and Brown, 2015). Trust is imperative when working with communities of color and/or low income because these communities have often been mistreated, ignored, and at times deliberately put in harm's way for the benefit of others (Bullard, 2008). Without trust, community members are less likely to attend capacity building sessions or even fully heed information distributed to the community (Goodall, 2015; Saegert et al., 2002; Park et al., 2018).

Critics of the bottom-up approach argue that this methodology is impractical due to the time and resources it takes to implement (Leviton, 2003; Casey, 2011). One way to mediate these impracticalities is to use a train-the-trainer model and equip local community leaders with the tools they need to "be trained" and "to train" their own leaders or community residents (Coffey et al., 2017). Doing this can increase stakeholder connections with community leaders and ensures both the credibility and reputability of the provided information (Swanson, 2013; Barnes and Schmitz, 2016). This increases the likelihood that the information will be used by community residents because the information is being delivered by a reputable source within the community. Community leaders often possess the ability to communicate across broad spectrums serving as a bridge between the community and the entities seeking to deliver information (Brooks, 2002; Wallace and Wolf, 2006).

Though there are many methods that can be used to transition from a top-down approach to a bottom-up approach, the approach presented in this book is grounded in participatory planning, and problem-based learning using a constructivist instructional method. Community leaders, practitioners, instructors/educators and evaluators who use this approach will obtain a better understanding of community values, morals, and overall ideals prior to entering the community.

BOX 1.1 K.A.P.S. FEATURED PRACTITIONER SPOTLIGHT 1

Pamela Hernandez, Ph.D.
Owner and Principal Researcher, EDUCO Research

What is your area of specialty?

I am an independent research consultant whose expertise is in qualitative research methods. I use research to build human capacity and social change.

How did you get into this work?

I became involved in this research because I wanted to be a part of social change. I want to learn more about the community and contribute to it. I also wanted to meet people and be proactively engaged.

How have you addressed the problems that marginalized communities face in your career?

I have helped marginalized communities build relationships with funding organizations. I have conducted multiple trainings that have helped to increase the capacity of native/non-native English speakers to become an advocate for their community.

What would you wish you could have done differently now that you looked back at the landscape of the field?

I do not have any regrets; every experience was a lesson learned that added to my value as a researcher. Through my experiences I learned that it is important to always follow your passion so that you can be a part of the process. My experiences helped me to identify my skillsets so that I can help other community members.

What is the biggest advice you have for other practitioners?

- Partner with organizations prior to entering a community
- Do not just give people links to [websites] do it [the task] with them
- Do not use jargon
- Allow people time to talk through issues and troubleshoot problems together

What are some activities you use to "self-care?"

- Putting a time limit on projects
- Exercise (two to three times a week)
- Be outdoors in nature
- Saying "No"!

"You have to be passionate about this work. So find what brings you passion. Say: 'This is my skillset and this is what I can do.'"

WORKING WITH MULTICULTURAL MULTI-HAZARD COMMUNITIES FROM THE BOTTOM-UP

Often researchers, practitioners, and public officials enter multicultural multi-hazard communities with set agenda items. In working with multicultural multi-hazard communities, it is important to enter the community as an empathetic advocate (Preece, 2004; Gormally, 2012). Empathetic advocates are those individuals who place their own agenda to the side and seek to "inform groups, including public agencies, of the condition, problems and outlook of the group he or she represents" (Davidoff, 1965: 288). The idea is to approach communities from a non-utilitarian and pluralistic perspective that encourages researchers and practitioners to consider a community's physical, economic, and social/societal attributes before applying a one-size-fits-all (utilitarian) model to a community (Fainstein and DeFilippis, 2015). To effectively operate within or on behalf of multicultural multi-hazard communities of color, it is important that the work is inclusive and seeks to improve as well as foster sustainable change (Berke et al., 2011). To become an empathetic advocate for a community, an individual should seek to L.E.E.D. by listening, educating, empowering, and driving change within the community (Semien, 2017).

When researchers and practitioners seek to listen first to the needs of the community, this allows residents space to identify the issues that they regularly face (Levin, 1992). As these issues are unveiled, researchers and practitioners will learn which areas they should focus on as well as which areas to focus less on and/or avoid. In multicultural multi-hazard communities, it is important to understand which areas should be completely avoided to ensure that researchers and practitioners do not upset members of the community regarding previous bad experiences (Ramasubramanian, 2015; Crawford et al., 2008). Providing an open space that is framed to empathetically interact with members of the community can help to relieve stress, build trust, and foster a learning environment (Preece, 2004; Anguiano et al., 2012; Gormally, 2012). During this process it is also important to ensure that every community member's voice is at the table, not just the community elites and leaders (Purdy, 2011; Ricketts, 2016). Ensuring that everyone is at the table includes those that may typically be invisible to those who do not immediately look for them (i.e., the single mother, the elderly, the disabled, the low income, etc.). In entering a multicultural multi-hazard community every voice and every story matters, even the ones others may consider insignificant. This type of listening and engagement allows for the development of strong relationships between the community and the researcher/practitioner/trainer.

FIGURE 1.1 A community hosted distribution site held after the "The Great Flood" of 2016 in Ascension Parish

Once community leaders, researchers, practitioners, educators, and trainers understand the challenges and successes of a community then it is time to educate. Educating from the perspective of bottom-up does not begin with the quick distribution of technical or academic knowledge, nor does it consist of a utilitarian approach (Macias, 2017; Brailas et al., 2017; Glantz, 2012). When researchers and practitioners listen first, the community unintentionally equips them with a unique set of tools that can now be used to ensure receptibility of technical and academic information (Wright, 2012; Whitehead et al., 2012). In entering a multicultural multi-hazard community, it is important to frame the technical and academic knowledge in the context of the community's experiences, such as through place-based examples (Semien and Nance, 2019; Whitehead et al., 2012). Using place-based examples and/or experiences provides community members with practical and relatable context for the application of knowledge/skills (Takvorian et al., 2012). In other words, the more relatable the information being taught, the more willing the individual will be to receive and apply the information to their life and community.

To further increase the receptibility of multicultural multi-hazard communities, it is important to ensure that distributed resources, information, and practices are culturally appropriate and equitably distributed (James et al., 2007; Bethel et al., 2013). "Culture is the conceptual system developed by a community or a society to structure the way people view the world" (SAMHSA, 2014: 14). The way people view the world can increase or decrease the way they receive as well as process technical or academic information. In using a bottom-up strategy it is important to ensure that researchers and practitioners are competent about the cultures within the communities they seek to offer support (Glantz, 2012; Schoch-Spana et. al., 2019). This will allow researchers to communicate on a level that can be easily received by the communities in which they work. In addition, it is also important that all information is equitably distributed to ensure that resources reach every individual living within the community. Equity ensures "that each person [that] has different circumstances [is] allocate[d] the exact resources and opportunities needed to reach an equal outcome" (MPH@GW, 2021). It is important to "meet people where they are" which may mean that information is distributed to schools, nursing homes, grocery stores, individual homes, and churches as compared to one time at a community meeting.

In working with multicultural multi-hazard communities, it is important to empower (equip) them with the tools and resources they need to fight for themselves (Glantz, 2012; Pranis, 2001; Butler and Adamowski, 2015). In seeking to empower communities, it is important that instructors use culturally competent, non-technical language adapted to fit the needs of the community. Once the tools and resources are adapted, then a train-the-trainer approach can be taken—this is a technique in which an instructor who has the technical knowledge teaches a community leader or a resident, then that leader or resident trains others (Tobias et al., 2012; Kaplan, 2000; Israel et. al., 2010). An example of this strategy is the Community Emergency Response Team (CERT) used by the Federal Emergency Management Agency (FEMA) in which community members are trained on how to respond to disasters. They are then sent out to train others (Flint and Brennan, 2006; Takahashi et al., 2014).

BOX 1.2 K.A.P.S. FEATURED COMMUNITY ACTIVIST 1

Nathanael Stephens
Chief Firefighter, Geismar, Louisiana

What is your primary role in your community?

I am the Chief firefighter at the Volunteer Geismar fire station.

Can you tell me a little bit about the history of the fire station?

Well, the fire station is a volunteer fire department. People from the community will volunteer as firefighters to support the residents in Geismar. We often function as a supporting agency to the industries if [there is] a chemical spill, fire, or explosion. Most chemical plants don't want fire trucks on their property because they have their own response team—so we just function as a support agency in the event that there is an additional need.

When did your work in the fire service begin and how long have you been in this field?

My career as a firefighter began when I worked in the chemical plant. I was trained to fight fires. My leadership abilities helped to increase my interest in fighting fires. I have been in [the] fire service for over 40 years. I have been the assistant chief and chief for about 20 years.

Why did you choose this field and how has your work impacted your community?

I watch the evolution of this community. The community is made up of slave descendants who once worked plots at the Waterloo Plantation. Those descendants bought the land and today they are being forced out because of industrialization and urbanization. Being a firefighter is more than just fighting fires, I chose this field because I wanted to do more for my community, the same community who gave so much to me. The people in this community are hardworking, good, caring people. My job is to ensure that those hardworking and good, caring people stay safe.

What are some resources that your fire station needs to be equipped to support a marginalized multi-hazard community like Geismar?

- Money to hire more personnel
- Training courses that focus on increasing the capacity of the staff and the community
- Incentives to obtain and retain volunteers
- Support for a young mentorship program

What advice can you offer other community leaders who are working as a volunteer in their communities?

One of the problems in the Geismar community is that the population has grown, and many people are not aware of the community preparedness and emergency alert systems. Community leaders should remember that no system is that good! If the people in the community don't know how to use the system, then the system will not work.

"People need to go to an official source for disaster related information and not just rely on information that they see on social media."

Human capital is the investment that people make within themselves in the form of professional education and training (Beaulieu, 2014; Adger and Brooks, 2003; Scandlyn et al., 2013). This form of capacity-building provides individuals with the technical and conceptual skills needed to be resilient (Haynes et al., 2019; Fordham et al., 2013). In the context of the K.A.P.S. framework, we use the definition of capacity building to mean "enabling those out on the margins to represent and defend their interest more effectively, not only within their own immediate contexts, but also globally" (Eade, 2007: 630). This method of empowerment creates opportunities for continuous learning that can equip the community with the tools needed to both learn and to help others within their community. These opportunities can help to build social networks, increase resiliency, and provide meaningful involvement (Aldrich and Meyer, 2015; Masterson et al., 2015). Communities know their weaknesses and when you equip those residents with tools and resources then they can build sustainably, incorporating equity, social justice, and democracy (Brooks, 2002; Allmendinger, 2009; Wallace and Wolf, 2006).

The final stage to becoming a community advocate is to drive change by ensuring that communities are "wearing their disaster K.A.P.S." Residents living with these communities know what ails them, but they often lack the support, resources, and political power to drive change within their communities (Thomas et al., 2009; Vaughan, 2020; Jenkins, 2009). Empathetic advocates can encourage communities to develop community-led councils, boards, and nonprofit organizations that can provide support for needed improvements in the community (Preece, 2004; Gormally, 2012). Increasing community stakeholder positions can aid in bringing a broad range of voices to the table with various interests such as healthy living, economic development, education, etc., and ensure that neighborhood changes are fair and just (Tewdwr-jones, 1998; Musso et al., 2002). As residents become more aware of and involved with aspects of their community that can bring political change, they gain continuous access to resources, information, and political relationships, which increases their resilience and ability to recover (Bullard and Wright, 2009; Pipa, 2006).

BOX 1.3 K.A.P.S. FEATURED MODEL 1

Communiversity
Beverly Wright, Ph.D.,
Founder and Executive Director, Deep South Center for Environmental Justice

Model in front of Definition

The Communiversity Model emphasizes a collaborative partnership between universities and communities.

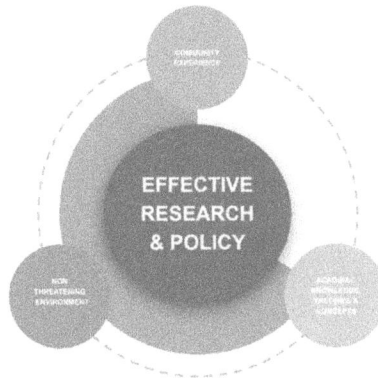

FIGURE 1.2 Effective research and policy

Model Summary

The Deep South Center for Environmental Justice (DSCEJ) has developed and embraces a model for community partnership that is called "**Communiversity.**" The community partnership promotes bilateral understanding and mutual respect between community residents and academicians. In the past, collaborative problem-solving attempts that included community residents and academicians were one-sided in terms of who controlled the dynamics of the interaction between the two, who was perceived as knowledgeable, and who benefited.

The essence of this approach is an acknowledgment that for effective research and policymaking, valuable community life experiences regarding environmental insult must be integrated with the theoretical knowledge of academic educators and researchers. Either group alone is less able to accomplish the goal of achieving environmental equity, but the coming together of the two in a non-threatening forum can encourage significant strides toward solutions. The DSCEJ has advanced the capital Communiversity Model with the formation of the DSCEJ Community Advisory Board (CAB). The board consists of grassroots community leaders, nonprofits, academics, and government officials along the Louisiana Mississippi River Chemical Corridor and the Gulf Coast Region.

Why Feature Communiversity?

The Communiversity Model has been tested over decades with dozens of different communities, and it has proven to be successful for both communities and researchers.

Learn more about the Communiversity model at: https://www.dscej.org/our-work/community-engagement

CHAPTER 2

Climate Resilience and Justice

....

CLIMATE RESILIENCE

We have entered, for the first time in the history of the planet, a 415 parts-per-million carbon dioxide atmosphere that threatens human resilience to climate change (Scripps Institution of Oceanography, 2019). The 197 nations that signed the Paris Agreement in 2015 committed to a coordinated global response to the threat of increasing carbon dioxide in the atmosphere (United Nations Framework Convention on Climate Change, 2021). Increased carbon dioxide—the primary cause—is associated with the warming of Earth's atmosphere beyond natural historic levels. Concentrations of atmospheric carbon dioxide measured at the Mauna Loa Observatory were 414.62 parts per million (ppm) in July 2020, and 416.96 ppm in July 2021 (NOAA Global Monitoring Laboratory, 2021). In contrast, the natural variation of carbon dioxide has been 175–300 ppm for the past 800,000 years (Gleick, 2019).

Another of Earth's vital signs—the increase in global surface temperature over time—is similarly dire. As of 2020, global temperature was 1.02 °C (1.84 °F) higher than the 1951–1980 average, and the years 2016 and 2020 were the warmest years on record since measurements began in 1880 (NASA, 2021a). According to NASA, "Direct observations made on and above Earth's surface show the planet's climate is significantly changing. Human activities are the primary driver of those changes" (NASA, 2021b).

Despite these findings, the scientific facts about climate change have been obscured, and it is important to understand why. The United States signed the Paris Agreement in 2016 but then withdrew in 2019, thus reneging on its formal commitment to respond to the global crisis, despite being the largest contributor of atmospheric carbon dioxide. The excuse given was that signing the agreement would undermine the US economy, the strongest economy in the world at the time. Decades

DOI: 10.4324/9781003177005-3

of false narratives had been promoted by the oil industry to justify such a position. In 2015, Columbia University and the Los Angeles Times reported that Exxon had known about the causes and dangers of climate change since the 1970s and that it was part of a sophisticated network of powerful actors that had blocked and mis-represented climate science to the public (Jerving et al., 2015). Climate change deniers proposed that global warming was natural and not the result of human activity. They accused climate scientists of making doomsday predictions and they spread misinformation to create the false impression that scientists disagreed about climate change (Elsasser and Dunlap, 2013).

As of 2021, the US re-joined the Paris Agreement and renewed its commitment. Whatever happens from here as the winds shift, it is important to understand the phenomena that we are all experiencing. The goal of this chapter is to summarize the physical and social impacts of climate change and human resilience to these changes, with special attention paid to climate justice; that is, to the distribution of climate change impacts.

THE ANTHROPOCENE

The "Anthropocene," so named by Paul J. Crutzen (Nobel Prize, 1995) and Eugene F. Stoermer in 2000, is the current geological period where it is recognized that humans have had, since World War II, profound impacts on the global environment. These impacts include the loss of biodiversity; the extinction of plant species, wild animals, and coral reefs; deforestation; ocean pollution; carbon pollution; and climate warming. Prominent scientists agree with both the scale and the cause of these changes, calling it biological annihilation produced by overpopulation and over-consumption by the rich (Ceballos et al., 2017).

The Anthropocene Working Group, a collection of internationally recognized earth scientists, voted overwhelmingly in 2019 to treat the Anthropocene as a formal chrono-stratigraphic unit within the Geological Time Scale, such as an epoch. The Group also voted overwhelmingly that the Anthropocene started in the mid-twentieth century of the Common Era, specifically during the emission of radio-nuclides that were spread across the globe by the atmospheric thermonuclear bomb tests that began in 1951.

While past military activities may have shifted the trajectory of the Earth's climate, many ongoing everyday activities have also contributed to the steady rise in atmospheric carbon, which triggers the warming effect and subsequent weather impacts and sea level rise. Chemicals that cause the atmosphere to warm are known as greenhouse gases (GHGs). These include water vapor (H_2O), carbon dioxide (CO_2), methane (CH_4), nitrous oxide (N_2O), ozone (O_3), and hydrofluorocarbons (HFCs). Scientists often combine all of the greenhouse gases into a carbon equivalent to make it easier to communicate the total impact. The following table lists the main activities of civilization that are causing climate change. Human activities have direct and indirect effects on the environment, which ultimately lead to climate change and reduced resilience to the impacts of climate change (Figure 2.1).

Human Activities	Primary Climate Effects
Power plants	Carbon dioxide emissions
Transportation/fossil fuel combustion	Carbon dioxide emissions
Industrialized agriculture/ranching	Methane and carbon dioxide emissions, reduced biodiversity, sediment transport
Industrialized fertilizers	Nitrous oxide emissions, heat sinks, riverine and oceanic dead zones
Deforestation, habitat loss	Carbon dioxide emissions, reduced forest stock, reduced biodiversity
Urbanization	Heat sinks, soil erosion
Oil drilling	Methane and carbon dioxide emissions
Natural gas	Methane emissions, air and water pollution
Landfills	Methane and nitrous oxide emissions
Cement production	Carbon dioxide emissions
Halocarbons and CFCs	Global warming, ozone layer depletion
Disruption of global chemical cycles	Global warming, melting glaciers, sea level rise, ocean acidification, oceanic dead zones

FIGURE 2.1 Connections between human activity and climate change

Sources: Trenberth (2018); Zalasiewicz et al., (2019); and Kelly (2019).

The first item in Figure 2.1, power plants, is a major fossil fuel emitter. The burning of fossil fuels is the largest human source of carbon dioxide emissions. Tremendous amounts of fossil fuel are burned during the mining of oil, coal, or natural gas. As the source fuel is transported to the power plant, fossil fuels are burned by trains, trucks, and ships. At the power plant, raw materials are burned as part of the process of creating electricity, thus emitting further carbon dioxide. The efficiency with which consumers use the resulting electricity depends on grid efficiency, housing quality, and land use decisions. Sprawling sub-divisions require more energy to heat and cool, more transportation to and from the city, and more concrete which burns additional fossil fuels during production. Poorly insulated structures are highly wasteful of energy. When power plants and structures are demolished, debris that is transported to landfills further adds to the carbon emissions burden. Carbon is emitted throughout the entire lifecycle of a power plant.

A host of human activities lead to climate change, and this impact is increasing as 83 million people are added to the planet annually (United Nations, 2017). At the consumption rate of the United States, four to five Earths would be needed to support life (Marks et al., 2006). Even at a normal rate of consumption, 1.5 Earths would be needed. Crops must double by 2050 to maintain global food security (Tilman et al., 2011). Thirty-six percent of global crop production is for livestock, while only

12 percent of the calories are for human consumption (Helne and Salonen, 2016). Global livestock operations emit a major portion of planetary carbon dioxide (Steinfeld et al., 2006). Massive fish farming destroys biodiversity and natural habitat, causing inbreeding, disease, parasites, and lice that spread to wild fish species (Worm et al., 2006). These human-caused habitat losses damage entire ecosystems—the web of life—on a scale beyond the fish farm. Half of all wild animals have disappeared in the last 40 years (Carrington, 2014), including many pollinator species (such as bees) that are critical to the pollination of 75 percent of the food crops eaten by humans (Bartomeus et al., 2014). In addition to being known as the Anthropocene, climate scientists have called this period the sixth mass extinction, in reference to this being the first loss of species caused by humans that follows the five previous periods of natural species decline (Cafaro, 2015). The most recent extinction was 66 million years ago.

The oceans are acidifying due to carbon emissions (30 percent of all carbon emissions end up in the ocean) and from agricultural run-off, which increases the acidity of the sea water and kills ocean life, especially phytoplankton which are an important food source and an important oxygen source (half of all oxygen on the planet is produced by phytoplankton) (Gruber et al., 2019). Plastic has already invaded all seafood. Approximately 11 million metric tons of plastic are dumped into the oceans every year (United Nations Clean Seas Campaign, 2021), and by 2050 the weight of all plastic will outweigh all fish (World Economic Forum, 2016). The plastic gets smaller over time but it never goes away; it becomes nanoplastic which is small enough to pass through the cell membrane. In Europe, it is estimated that 11,000 pieces of plastic are eaten per year in fish. Researchers from Stanford University long ago predicted the collapse of all fisheries by 2048 (Worm et al., 2006). Food insecurity will be a primary impact of climate change. While food insecurity may manifest locally, it is tied to reductions in agricultural yields at the regional level, which are tied to temperature rise, drought, and ecosystem change at the global level (Figure 2.2).

Non-human activities also cause climate change. Underground frozen methane in the Arctic region is bubbling to the surface as the permafrost melts, causing an explosion hazard and contributing to climate change. Methane is a greenhouse gas that is 20 times stronger than carbon dioxide, so it does far more damage to the climate when released. The non-stop warming is causing the seas to rise. Economists estimate that $106 billion in US coastal property will be literally underwater by 2050 (Risky Business, 2014).

It has taken scientists decades to figure out the sources, causes, and significance of climate change. The leading international body of scientists is the Intergovernmental Panel on Climate Change (IPCC), a body of the United Nations founded in 1988 and with headquarters in Geneva, Switzerland. The IPCC assesses the state of the science, issues special reports, and develops policy options for adaptation and mitigation of climate change effects. Because of the decades of delay in taking action in the US, mitigation is no longer believed to be practicable. We must adapt to the massive changes that are already in process.

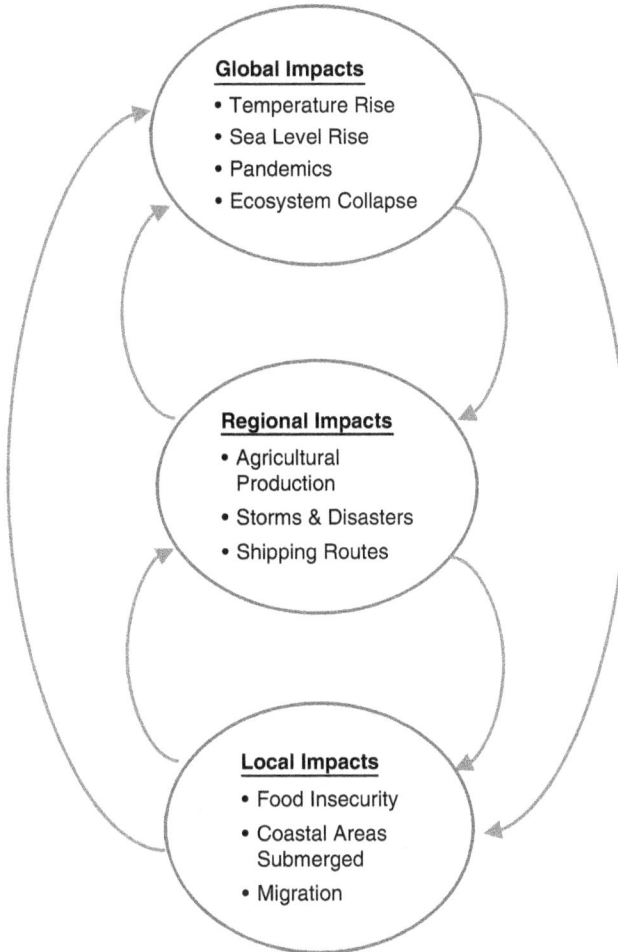

FIGURE 2.2 Visualization of relationships between the local, regional, and global impacts of climate change

The effects of climate changes are apparent in the intensity and frequency of natural disasters. In 2020, recording-breaking wildfires burned 4 million acres in California, doubling the previous record of 2 million acres set in 2018. The Gulf and Atlantic coasts saw a record-breaking 30 tropical storms and hurricanes, ten of which occurred in a single month (September), and it was the fifth year in a row to have a Category 5 hurricane (the strongest). Also in 2020 in the US, there were three major tornado outbreaks, two major hail storms, drought, severe weather, and dam failures caused by rainfall flooding, and a record-breaking heatwave in Phoenix (144 days at 100 °F and 90 °F on November 16) (Thompson, 2020). Overall, there were 22 disasters that caused $1 billion or more in damage each, resulting in a total annual cost of $95 billion and 262 deaths. According to the National Oceanic and Atmospheric Administration (Frank, 2021), "2020 stands head and shoulders above all other years in regard to the number of billion-dollar disasters … reflecting the increasing costs of climate change."

CLIMATE JUSTICE

Climate change is a justice issue for three reasons. First, its causes are driven by social inequalities: most politically, culturally, and economically marginalized communities and nations use vastly less fossil fuel-based energy. Second, the rich and poor feel its impacts unequally; this is true locally, nationally, and globally. Third, policies designed to manage climate change – including renewable energy sources, adaptation measures, and geoengineering schemes – will have starkly unequal impacts within and across societies. This is in part because decision-making processes for emissions reductions and adaptation policies tend to exclude the politically marginalized.

(Harlan et al., 2015: 1)

The impacts of climate change are horrific in scale and scope. But environmental catastrophes have existed all around us for many decades. Systems of war, genocide, colonialism, slavery, human trafficking, and hatred have produced racial, ethnic, and economic hierarchies, with those at the bottom being continuously oppressed. Some of the tools of continuous oppression include policing and mass incarceration, school systems, housing, and environmental racism. Each of these systems traps a large percentage of people of color, immigrants, poor people, and others into an oppressed condition. For example, in 2018 Black men were incarcerated at a rate 5.8 times higher than white men (Carson, 2020).

The outcomes of oppression lead to a cycle of marginalization. For example, poor Black people in the South and the North were forced to live in bottomlands, redlined areas, and other undesirable locations, keeping more desirable areas for whites. This reduced the resilience of marginalized populations to climate-induced flooding. Once geographically segregated, polluting plants, landfills, and other hazardous industries eventually located next door to the marginalized settlements because of their lack of political power, which permanently depressed poor people's property values and financially trapped them.

Many cities and homes have been built in areas vulnerable to disaster, such as along coastlines and floodplains, near forests, and in deserts. Building codes, zoning laws, and construction standards have generally been only partially protective against natural hazards. Furthermore, as climate change has quietly worsened, the damage caused by natural hazards has grown exponentially. This upward trend covers droughts, wildfires, floods, winter storms, freezes, severe storms, and tropical cyclones. Some hazards have reached a tipping point whereby most of the population has become consciously aware of the increasing risk and are taking action. These areas include, for example, the Southeast Louisiana region where hurricanes are increasing, land is disappearing at an alarming rate due to human activities, and mass population movement has already begun. They also include California where wildfires now devastate the state each year.

To make matters worse, the Gulf Coast has the fastest rate of sea level rise in the US. Global sea level is expected to rise by at least one foot by 2100 under the best greenhouse gas emissions scenario; and by 8.2 feet under the worst-case scenario (Sweet et al., 2017). As 40 percent of the US population lives in coastal areas, more and more communities will find themselves impacted by some combination of worsening natural hazards, land loss, and sea level rise. Environmental displacement, climate gentrification, and climate-induced migration are some of the terms being used to describe this emerging situation.

In addition to natural hazards, some communities face human-made environmental hazards such as petrochemical facilities, oil and gas plants, incinerators, hazardous waste landfills, sewage plants, concrete plants, and high diesel truck traffic, among others. These "fenceline" communities are comprised primarily of people of color, indigenous, and low-income/poor people. Nationwide, fenceline communities experience disproportionate burdens of exposure to pollution, increased health risks, and environmental health disparities (Wilson, 2009). Race is the strongest indicator of health risk in fenceline communities (APHA, 2019), leading to use of the term "environmental racism" to describe this phenomenon. In 2008, approximately 56 percent of the population living near Toxic Release Inventory facilities were people of color (Bullard, 2008). Toxic Release Inventory facilities represent the major pollution producing facilities in the US.

Because of the health consequences of disproportionate exposure, the American Public Health Association calls these environmental injustices both a structural public health issue and a human rights issue. These communities are also disproportionately impacted by climate-induced hazards, and because of their socioeconomic position they are less able to mitigate impacts or escape from harm. This book incorporates climate and environmental justice issues into a disaster planning and hazard mitigation framework. With the increasing intensity and frequency of climate-induced hazards everywhere, fenceline communities are at risk of being left behind. Planning for climate change means planning for those who are most at risk.

BOX 2.1 K.A.P.S. FEATURED MODEL 2

Participatory Sanitation

Earthea Nance, Ph.D.
Environmental Protection Agency Region 6 Administrator

Model Definition and Summary

Sustainable infrastructure is critical for both resilience and justice. In the developing world, the lack of basic water and sanitation services for over 3 billion people still contributes to disease, death, low productivity, and poor school attendance (especially for girls).

Brazil is a critical case for examining the role of technical innovation, community participation, and discourse in transforming the sanitation sector on a large scale. Known locally as condominial sewers, the new technology is making sanitation services more inclusive. Condominial sewers were installed with intense community involvement since the 1980s and were highly controversial initially because they violated infrastructure norms.

The systems reduced costs by using shallow trench depths and small diameter pipes, and by their location in backyards, front yards, sidewalks, alleys, paths, and lanes instead of paved streets. By co-producing the systems with communities, activist engineers increased sewer access for the poor from 21 percent in 1980 to 80–100 percent in 2020 for the cities of Brasilia and Salvador Bahia. Engineers and officials promoted the innovation to attract funding, gain community interest, and change infrastructure rules to support universal service. Today the World Bank is taking the innovation to other countries.

FIGURE 2.3 Visualization of sanitation in Brazil

Why Feature Participatory Sanitation?

The Participatory Sanitation Model offers proof that participatory approaches are effective and can increase the resilience of low-income communities on a large scale.

Learn more about the Participatory Sanitation Model at: Earthea Nance (2012). Engineers and Communities: Transforming Sanitation in Contemporary Brazil, Lanham, MD: Lexington Books. https://rowman. com/ISBN/9780739179284.

CHAPTER 3

Social Construct of Vulnerability

....

This chapter presents a summary of the social and institutional sources of vulnerability.

SOCIAL SOURCES OF DISASTER VULNERABILITY

The social construction of disasters is a mainstay of the disaster planning field (Hewitt, 1983; Wijkman and Timberlake, 1984; Wisner, 1984). Rather than being purely natural, an array of social forces is widely recognized as creating disaster vulnerabilities in different groups. These social factors are economic, political, societal, and cultural.

Risk build-up involves social and economic processes that create evolving risk over long time periods, resulting in catastrophic risk (Tierney, 2014: 125). For example, urban development "growth machines" promote residential, commercial, and industrial development by any means necessary, including loosening environmental and safety regulations and allowing development in high-hazard areas. This pattern is nearly ubiquitous across the United States. Urban developers, industrialists, and their supportive elected officials literally bank on the fact that federal subsidies and federal response and recovery funds will pay for many of the losses. When this happens, government funds are privatized into profits and any risks and losses are socialized, that is, covered by the public.

The systemic power of pro-growth actors is enhanced when they join forces with elected officials to advance their own profit-seeking agendas. Pro-growth groups are most often comprised of land developers, real estate interests, banks, key industries, and elite businesses. They form durable alignments with political actors based on promoting a discourse of job creation, tax incentives, and increased community investments (Molotch, 1976; Logan and Molotch, 1987; Stone, 1980). These pro-growth activities increase vulnerability to disaster by creating extreme pressure to expand development in high-hazard areas. The pressure to develop can be so high

DOI: 10.4324/9781003177005-4

there have been many instances of fraud in conducting building inspections, preparing geological reports, redefining the hazard, calculating benefits and costs, and disregarding safe building requirements (Tierney 2014: 136–139).

Culture has been nearly ignored as part of the social construction of vulnerability (Cannon, 2015: 88). In addition to cultural beliefs, cultural values, attitudes, and behaviors, organizational cultures associated with disaster response and recovery also count as a cultural force that constructs vulnerability.

A range of socioeconomic factors drive the disaster vulnerability of individuals and groups (Figure 3.1). Overall, being dependent on others for anything can make one vulnerable; however, having a trusted community, family, or network can overcome that vulnerability. Not having enough resources can make one vulnerable, but having other sources to draw from, such as government disaster aid, can reduce that vulnerability. Being non-white in the US makes many people continuously vulnerable because of institutionalized racism.

The same social forces of risk production are evident in countries outside the United States (Tierney, 2014: 150). The severity of disasters is associated with a nation's position in the global economy. National political power, level of development, history of colonization, imposition of structure adjustment measures, trade agreements, and the effects of globalization are international forces related to disaster vulnerability. These international forces create local conditions such as rapid urbanization, informal settlements, income inequality, and environmental degradation that translate to increased disaster vulnerability. The power and predictability of social forces cannot be understated.

As dependable as the social forces listed in Figure 3.1 are at determining vulnerability, less studied are how vulnerability plays out during and after disasters. The static factors in Figure 3.1 do not explain patterns of disaster vulnerability established by organizations, rules, policies, and via institutional actions taken during disaster recovery and mitigation. These institutional sources of vulnerability are outlined in the next section.

INSTITUTIONAL SOURCES OF DISASTER VULNERABILITY

Benefit-Cost Analysis

Benefit-cost analysis (BCA) is a federal rule that requires all disaster funding to be economically efficient. The origin of the rule is President Reagan's Executive Order 12866. Some economically efficient allocations are fairer than others (less regressive). In Harris County, Texas benefit-cost analysis has efficiently produced inequitable flood protection outcomes, with lower income groups and people of color exposed to higher environmental risks than whiter and wealthier groups. The majority of flood protection funding in Harris County has been federal, and all of it had to pass federal benefit-cost criteria. The inequity that exists on the ground today is, by definition, economically efficient. Whiter and wealthier segments of the Harris County population have benefitted from the BCA approach and have continued to receive

Socioeconomic Factor	Definition
Income	In general, low-income people are more vulnerable when disaster strikes and less able to recover; lack of resources reduces options available in disaster.
Poverty	In general, people in poverty are at risk of becoming homeless in a disaster, have few resources with which to recover; increased vulnerability, and a higher chance of death.
Social class/status	In general, people of low social class will be discriminated against during a disaster, increasing their vulnerability and reducing their access to resources.
Race	In general, non-white people will be discriminated against during a disaster, experience more vulnerability, and have a harder time recovering.
Ethnicity	In general, people of non-European ethnicity will be discriminated against during a disaster, experience more vulnerability, and have a harder time recovering.
Culture	In general, many cultural beliefs are grounded in a historical connection to land, which mediates disaster response.
Physical ability	In general, physically challenging disaster preparations such as boarding up windows are difficult for people with limited ability, which increases their vulnerability.
Disability	In general, differently abled people might need more assistance during a disaster, which increases their vulnerability.
Language competency	In general, the lack of language justice keeps non-English speakers vulnerable to disasters.
Social networks/ social capital	In general, people with few relationships have less social capital (trust, reciprocity, cooperation), which increases vulnerability.
Gender	In general, women are more vulnerable to disaster because of their lower income and social status, and because they may be caring for others.
Household composition	In general, more women, elders, and children are associated with vulnerability to disaster because these groups are more vulnerable due to income, physical ability, and social status.
Home ownership	In general, homeowners are less vulnerable because of income, home equity, and federal programs for owners.
Age	In general, elderly people struggle during and after disaster and suffer high rates of injury and death.

FIGURE 3.1 Socioeconomic factors that drive disaster vulnerability

downstream benefits such as community development, high property values, and easier eligibility for disaster assistance to maintain their property values. Vulnerable segments of the population have suffered physically, mentally, and economically. This outcome is not the only possible economically efficient outcome. One only must look at other OECD countries for plenty of examples showing it is possible to efficiently achieve universal coverage for life safety services such as drinking water, firefighting, and flood protection. The inequities propagated by the BCA rule have created questions of fairness, racism, and human rights in disasters (Nance, 2021).

Eligibility Rules

FEMA programs supplement BCA analysis with eligibility rules. Low-income homeowners often lack flood insurance, which means they do not have a documented flood damage history. Without recorded damage history, their BCA ratio will come out low and will result in an insufficient award. Those not insured will be ineligible for Flood Mitigation Assistance (FMA) or Hazard Mitigation Grant Program (HMGP) funding unless the structure is substantially damaged. If substantially damaged and insured, they will be eligible for a buyout but not eligible for elevation or reconstruction. Low-to-moderate income (LMI) areas often comprise properties that lack clear title, properties with non-traditional mortgages, heavily leveraged properties, and properties that lack compliance with flood insurance requirements from previous grants. All these conditions make many LMI properties ineligible (or only eligible for small awards), which means that the conditions in which low-income people live are systematically used to deny their eligibility for disaster resources. Moreover, the needs of renters are not adequately addressed in FEMA programs (Nance, 2021).

Property Damage Metric

The required use of property damage as a metric in benefit-cost analysis to determine the amount of a FEMA award is discriminatory on its face and in practice. Initial damage estimates conducted after a disaster can be incorrect or manipulated, especially when the sheer number of damaged homes is enormous and there are not enough trained estimators. For low-income properties, a damage estimate can result in condemnation of the property if the estimator decides that the damage was not caused by the disaster. Property damage estimates are almost impossible to challenge, especially for low-income residents. Despite the potential inaccuracy of property damage estimates, they play a critical role in determining both eligibility and award amount. Damage estimates can be used to deny eligibility for low-income residents, and their required use in BCA privileges wealthier property owners in the awarding of funds. Wealthy property owners have more property value to lose, which makes it easier to get a high BCA and a larger award. The resulting inequity contributes to the vulnerability of lower income disaster victims (Nance, 2021).

Relocation

Studies show that disaster relocation programs are more disruptive for homeowners in black and brown communities than for homeowners in white or affluent neighborhoods. Homeowners from more privileged neighborhoods resettle closer to both their flood prone homes and to one another, thus helping to preserve the social as well as economic value of the home, whereas homeowners from less privileged areas end up farther away from both. Residents moving from a neighborhood where buyout prices average $80,000 end up three times farther from their original home than those moving from a neighborhood where buyout prices averaged $280,000, and they end up nearly twice as far from neighbors resettling through the same program (Nance, 2021; Elliott et al., 2021).

Institutionalized Inequity

Traditional patterns of inequity have remained despite substantial attempts to end it, not by FEMA, but by local practitioners. After Katrina, New Orleans had FEMA mitigation funds and an equity-focused mitigation office that fought hard for equity, but that was not enough to overcome inequitable outcomes that resulted from using FEMA programs. After Harvey, Harris County had data, metrics, policy, votes, and dedicated funds, but that was not enough to overcome inequitable outcomes associated with using FEMA programs. FEMA programs have institutionalized a pattern of inequity in disaster response and mitigation that has become normal (Rice University, 2018). It is normal for cities and counties to create a list of inequitable projects, for the state to approve those projects because they meet benefit-cost criteria, and for FEMA to approve and fund the projects. Anyone who critiques these decisions on the grounds of inequity or injustice must fight an entire system. In the Deep South and the Gulf Coast, where institutionalized racism and poverty are compounded by exceptional vulnerability to sea level rise, flooding, extreme heat, hurricanes, and other hazards, these are real struggles (Nance, 2010).

Sacrifice Zones

The demand for equity in floodplain management, environmental protection, disaster response, and climate change resilience is rising sharply. The population is looking to the government, especially to FEMA, for leadership on how to stay safe and productive while experiencing an onslaught of disasters. Low-income neighborhoods and people of color often live in sacrifice zones where they simultaneously experience worsening flooding, worsening environmental quality, and worsening health. A recent study of Hurricane Harvey found storm-induced flooding was significantly greater in Houston neighborhoods that had a higher proportion of Black and socioeconomically deprived residents. A nationwide study found that climate change is increasing the number of bad air days and posing significant health threats, including cardiovascular, respiratory allergies, and asthma, with an unequal burden falling on low income and people of color households who are exposed to more hazards.

Researchers found that in counties badly hit by natural disasters (areas with at least $10 billion in damages), white communities *gained* an average $126,000 in wealth following the damage and recovery efforts. Communities of color *lost* up to $29,000 on average in personal wealth following events like hurricanes and wildfires (Howell and Elliott, 2018). Results like these only confirm that FEMA's programs are not serving the public interest. On the contrary, the data show that FEMA's programs are serving whiter and wealthier segments of the population, even as underserved and marginalized segments of the population are less resilient to worsening disasters and are receiving less assistance (Nance, 2021).

Lack of Research

There is a growing amount of data about the bias of FEMA programs toward whiter and wealthier populations, however the research community has not addressed this widespread problem with the full energy and attention that it deserves. Vulnerable communities have complained for years about being left behind. The entire world watched as the US government systematically failed vulnerable people in Hurricane Katrina, and then again in Hurricane Maria. Other instances, such as Hurricane Laura, had less news coverage but still displayed the same pattern. Scholars recommend five ways to conduct better research on flood equity: 1) collect data on the types of hazards experienced by vulnerable populations, 2) use metrics that are unbiased and that include well-being, 3) analyze mechanisms that perpetuate inequality, 4) examine those who profit from the current system, and 5) broaden participation in hazards research (Hino and Nance, 2021).

Disproportionate Prioritization

In places like New Orleans, Houston, and Miami, nearly every structure is at risk of flooding, regardless of whether it is inside a flood zone, so most structures should be eligible for funding, especially after a large disaster. These cities also have many repetitive loss structures that are all eligible for funding. Nevertheless, it is difficult to rationally prioritize and distribute FEMA funds in these conditions because eligibility is hard to prove yet almost everyone should be eligible. In this situation, political clout often invades the prioritization process. Several recent publications have gathered data showing disproportionate eligibility, with wealthier and whiter areas being significantly more eligible for FEMA funds (Nance, 2021; Dreier, 2021; Dreier and Tran, 2021).

State Bias

By law, federal programs are not designed for communities; they are designed for states. FEMA rules do not adapt to local reality, especially the realities of socioeconomic marginalization, cumulative risk, repeated disasters, and state-established sacrifice zones like the Houston Ship Channel and the Mississippi River Chemical Corridor. It is up to states to adapt to the local reality, but this frequently breaks down. Unlike communities, states have authority to establish and play by their own limited rules for distributing FEMA funds. For example, states can delay payment or slow down processing, they can create competing programs, and they can positively work against some cities, even the most devastated. All these tactics were used against New Orleans during Hurricane Katrina. States do not equally represent all communities. States (and communities) use FEMA programs to carry out their development priorities, which are subject to pressure from corporations and not necessarily public needs (Nance, 2010; Nance 2021).

Targeted for Fraud

FEMA erects tremendous barriers to prevent fraud and bureaucratic risk, while doing next to nothing to prevent contractor fraud, which is extensive. The suspicion of fraud was most obvious in FEMA responses to New Orleans and Puerto Rico, both with high populations of black and brown applicants. Vulnerable people struck by disaster are often desperately in need of help, but this is not the same thing as being capable of fraud. The obstacles created to prevent fraud can cause positive harm to the most vulnerable people (Nance, 2021).

Types of Risk

FEMA funds do not cover all types of risk, especially the types of risk often experienced by poor, BIPOC, and elderly communities. These include excess flooding that results from the accumulation of deferred maintenance of urban drainage systems, cumulative structure damage that results from a lack of access to FEMA assistance in past disasters and which affects future eligibility, excess flood risk that results from a lack of infrastructure in marginalized communities, and residual flood risk outside the FEMA flood zone (Nance, 2021).

Listed and Zoned Properties

FEMA hazard mitigation assistance is designed to serve individual properties that are either listed (on RL or SRL lists) or zoned (inside the 100-year flood zone). To be listed requires having flood insurance, yet people outside the flood zone often do not think they need flood insurance or cannot afford flood insurance. This limited approach encourages local communities to ignore non-listed or non-zoned properties still at risk, many of which are low-income and more vulnerable (Nance, 2021; Nance, 2009).

Matching Funds

FEMA mitigation programs are structurally unsound because they only provide funds to entities (states, cities, and individuals) that already have access to start-up capital or matching funds, which again privileges wealthier groups. Every aspect of disaster programs reward people who are already advantaged. Some special programs do exist for low-income disaster victims, but these do not cover the volume of need (Nance, 2021; Nance, 2009).

Bureaucratic Inefficiency

Unnecessary layers of review of all FEMA applications at both state and federal levels have resulted in years of delay in distributing desperately needed funds. Applications are routinely audited and inspected at unreasonable levels. Residents often ask if FEMA reviewers are intensely searching for fraud or if they are trying to avoid giving awards to certain people. FEMA's review process creates unconscionable delays that affect thousands of people in the impacted community, including financial loss and mental anguish. The harm is worse for poorer, BIPOC, and elderly population segments. Delays have been so long as to cause increases in construction cost estimates, requiring resubmittal of the application; and to cause people to lose their homeowner's insurance due to the appearance of inaction. Bureaucratic inefficiencies in FEMA programs have resulted in an excessive waste of staff time, salaries, travel and equipment expenses, and other resources expended by local government to implement FEMA programs (Nance, 2021; Nance, 2009).

Lack of Communication

Lack of direct communication between FEMA and the affected community (communities are only allowed to talk to the State) also contributes to ongoing confusion and frustration about the status of FEMA applications. Even though federal programs are already spelled out in publicly available program guidance, the actual rules are redefined by the state—and many of these rules and procedures are not fully available to local officials and the public. The gap in program knowledge and the lack of transparency creates further delays and frustration. The 2021 surprise regarding the Texas General Land Office's decision not to fund Harris County and Houston is one example (Nance, 2021; Despart and Scherer, 2021; Nance, 2009).

Lack of Transparency

There is no direct link between FEMA announcements of funding allocations (which typically get national news coverage) and actual availability of FEMA funds at the state or local level. It is not possible to locate funds at any given time, so it is not possible to report anything to the community. This lack of accountability and lack of transparency makes it difficult to impossible for poorer residents (who do not have access to other funds) to plan their recovery (Nance, 2021; Nance, 2010).

Incentive Structure

There exist hidden incentives for states to delay distribution of funds to a municipality, such as the financial interest earned on funds received; the ability to create and promote programs that deliver a higher number of small awards over a lower number of large awards; and the ability to limit local-level discretion in establishing and meeting policy objectives, including equity objectives. All three of these tactics were applied in New Orleans after Hurricane Katrina, where the local political environment clashed with the state and federal environments. People of color and low-income suffered because of this power and incentive structure. Federal disaster policy does not cover disaster victims who are marginalized by power and incentive structures in place at the time of disaster. Federal disaster policies disproportionately affect vulnerable populations. The COVID-19 pandemic is an example of a disaster where the federal government made direct transfers instead of going through the state, for the purpose of bypassing the incentive structure and reaching those most vulnerable (Nance, 2021; Nance, 2010).

BOX 3.1 K.A.P.S. FEATURED MODEL 3

Equitable Flood Management
Jamila Johnson, PE, CFM
Walter P. Moore

Model Definition

The idea of Equitable Flood Management is that the resources of city, state, and federal agencies are used to reduce the risk of flood loss for all members of the community. The purpose of Equitable Flood Management is for the entire population to avoid and better recover from floods. The approach ensures that everyone gets the service they need while recognizing that not everybody needs the same thing. In some neighborhoods, the focus may be on helping people access their insurance benefits. For those without insurance, the focus may be on helping people access individual assistance and other programs.

Model Summary

Equitable Flood Management targets flood prone areas, identifies needs, plans for addressing those needs both before and after a flood, prioritizes the needs, and leverages local, state, and federal resources. The model requires continuous progress on mitigation and a plan for what to do after a flood. Current models do not do this holistically.

Two communities in Houston, Texas with repeated floods are Meyerland and Kashmere Gardens. Meyerland has 95 percent flood insurance support and is upper middle class, but they have problems too. They often request assistance in accessing their insurance benefits, obtaining temporary living arrangements, learning how to personally mitigate their property, and obtaining grant funding if possible. Over time these folks are all okay; they recover, self-mitigate, and move on.

Kashmere Gardens, on the other hand, has less than 25 percent flood insurance support, mostly low-to-moderate income, and issues that are relatively more significant than Meyerland. They often do not have access to temporary living arrangements so they end up in shelters. They often lose all their worldly possessions, including car and home, and they often do not recover for years and years. They receive no money from flood insurance and only small amounts of individual assistance from FEMA, which is not enough to recover. Temporary living expenses are high, and even with disaster programs there are situations where people rely on all their personal resources to make it. In this neighborhood, a flood event is life changing. Families lose everything, become homeless, and slowly reestablish themselves over time. How to address these very different needs in all areas of the city is what Equitable Floodplain Management is about.

Why Feature Equitable Flood Management?

The Equitable Flood Management approach would serve vulnerable communities who have not been served under conventional flood management models.

Learn more about the Equitable Flood Management at:

Water Rising: Equitable Approaches to Urban Flooding, http://uswateralliance.org/sites/uswateralliance.org/files/publications/Final_USWA_Water%20Rising_0.pdf

Complete Communities Plans for Kashmere and Acres Home Living with Water, City of Houston

Learn More about Jamila Johnson at https://www.walterpmoore.com/jamila-johnson

PART II

The K.A.P.S. Model

....

For decades, researchers have observed, assessed, and reported results regarding the experiences of individuals living in multi-hazard and socially vulnerable communities. However, few researchers have used their findings to directly increase the capacity of the individuals who live, work, and play in these communities. While these groups are the most researched, they are typically the least educated on mitigation and prevention behavioral changes needed to cope throughout the disaster life cycle (mitigation, preparedness, response, and recovery). There is a direct ethical disparity that allows scholars to continuously research these groups without providing substantial action to support the challenges these groups face. To bridge this gap, Part II of the book seeks to present the K.A.P.S. capital Model as one method to collaboratively turn knowledge into action through education.

Scholars like Muttarak and Lutz (2014) have shown that disaster education is important for reducing vulnerability and increasing resilience; this resource is often limited for vulnerable populations (Faupel et al., 1992; Lindholm et al., 2015; Morrow, 1999). While we recognize that disaster education alone cannot solve these disparities, studies like Sutton and Tierney (2006) have indicated that increasing mitigation and preparedness measures of the household can greatly reduce the impacts of disasters. The next section seeks to provide a series of educational frameworks that can help the individual household mitigate and prepare for disaster using disaster education as a form of capacity building.

There are few handbooks available to collectively guide disaster planners, practitioners, researchers, and community leaders on best practices for educating high-risk communities. The guiding principle outlined in this book is to tailor educational content to the community and to use practical, constructivist (hands-on) teaching

DOI: 10.4324/9781003177005-5

techniques to facilitate discussion as well as skill building activities (Frankenberg et al., 2013; Khalid and Azeem, 2012; Kim, 2005). The next two chapters in this Part address the following: Chapter 4: Knowledge and Attitude, and Chapter 5: Preparedness and Skills. Each chapter is designed in a manner that 1) explains the importance of incorporating each topic and 2) provides instructional techniques for presenting this information to high-risk communities.

CHAPTER 4

Applying the Knowledge and Attitudes in K.A.P.S.

....

Columbia University disaster research center released a statement that read "Disaster preparedness is [not just about] stockpiles of water and batteries and survival, it is about what people know, what they think, and who they trust" (National Center for Disaster Preparedness, 2020). In teaching the community to prepare for a disaster, it is imperative to not only focus on the physical aspects of preparedness but also to equip the community with the tools they need to acquire knowledge, critically decide, and build a strong trustworthy social network with a positive attitude.

This chapter focuses on applying the knowledge and attitudes in K.A.P.S. within communities by (1) unpacking the critical aspects of disaster knowledge and having a positive attitude toward disasters, (2) providing concepts that should be taught within instructional workshops, and (3) providing methods to teach knowledge and attitudes.

K (KNOWLEDGE) IN K.A.P.S.

While we recognize that educational trainings like K.A.P.S. are only one step to increasing community resilience, it is an imperative one as Sir Francis Bacon once said "scientia potestas est" meaning "knowledge is power" (García, 2001). This is a critical statement, for marginalized communities as individuals living within these communities are consistently threatened by hazards and disasters. These same individuals often lack the technical knowledge needed to understand their susceptibility, vulnerabilities, and risk to a disaster. They typically rely heavily on adaptive behavior acquired from the generational passing on of traditional and local knowledge (Kelman et al., 2012). Sutton and Tierney (2006) indicated that knowledge is one of the keys to prepare, respond, and recover from a disaster and without basic knowledge, the susceptibility of an individual to a hazard increases. This chapter seeks to examine the role that knowledge plays in marginalized communities, provide methods to encourage

DOI: 10.4324/9781003177005-6

attitude changes, and provide a set of instructional tools that can be adapted to train marginalized communities on hazards and disasters.

Types of Knowledge

Knowledge as defined by the *Oxford English Dictionary* (1989) is simply "the facts, information, and skills acquired by a person through experience or education." While the origin of knowledge transcends disciplines, epistemological philosophers have followed the lead of Kant's theory who recognized there are two sources for acquiring knowledge: *posterior*, knowledge derived from experience, and *a priori* knowledge derived before an experience (Bruce, 2020; Kitcher, 1980; Fieser, 2009). In hazard and disaster research we refer to the acquisition of knowledge as information acquired from technical (scientific) knowledge or local (indigenous) knowledge (Mazza, 2002; Dekens, 2007; Corburn, 2003).

Technical Knowledge (also known as Scientific Knowledge) is the body of information derived from scientific research and/or best practices obtained from the work of practitioners (Mazza, 2002; Guy, 2006). In many cases technical knowledge relies heavily on researchers and practitioners to support claims and ideas (Eliasson, 2000; Mazza, 2002). This information is often obtained from research studies or formal programmatic studies authored by academic scholars, practitioners, or governmental entities. The methodology used to obtain and justify this knowledge acquisition is typically obtained by applying the scientific method (Mäntysalo, 2005). This five-method process is designed to answer a question through justification. This strenuous process of questioning, testing, retesting, and extensive validation by outside scholars serves as the basis of knowledge presented to the general public—making it difficult to discredit without going back through this process. The problem with this information is that it leaves out local (indigenous) knowledge (Makondo and Thomas, 2018).

Local (Indigenous) Knowledge (also known as Traditional Ecological Knowledge, TEK) is the body of information acquired through generational dialogues, lived experiences, rituals, traditions, and institutions (Kelman et al., 2012; Makondo and Thomas, 2018). Another name for local (indigenous) knowledge is traditional ecological knowledge described by Berkes et al. (2000: 1252) as "knowledge, practice, and belief, that evolve by adaptive processes, handed down through generations by cultural transmission, about the relationship of living beings with one another and with their environment." In other words, it is the cultural and historical information passed from a parent to a child, a grandparent to a grandchild, and a community elder to a young person (Warburton and McLaughlin, 2007; Yang and Warburton, 2018). The fields of ethnography and preservation have helped to solidify the importance of addressing and protecting, the generational passing of information, specifically as it relates to a community's ability to adapt to environmental changes (Warburton and McLaughlin, 2007). Take for example the small multi-hazard community of St. James, Louisiana located along the Mississippi River. Many of the

African American population are the direct descendants of slaves living on the same plantation lands their ancestors once worked as slaves.

Today those areas are congested with a new form of plantation called industrialization where massive petrochemical plants fill the air, soil, and water with pollutants. Environmental activists like Sharon Lavigne work tirelessly to pass down the traditions of her community while also raising awareness of the environmental hazards destroying key cultural assets such as the unmarked graves of her African Ancestors (Blanks et al., 2021). She uses her local knowledge along with the power of her voice to build awareness needed to protect cultural assets and solicit support for the needs of her community, while holding leaders accountable for their actions (Stop Formosa Plastics, n.d.). Learn more about Sharon Lavigne and Rise St. James in Box 4.1. Local knowledge is a critical component needed to foster relationships, effectively communicate with the community, and increase a community's resilience capacity.

FIGURE 4.1 Image of a home and a chemical plant in Norco, Louisiana

Resilience Capacity

Resilience capacity can be defined as "the ability of people, households, communities and institutions to prepare for, respond to and recover from shocks and stresses prompted by the sources of resilience that enable protected or improved well-being outcomes" (Vaughan, 2018: 1). There are three types of resilience capacities: absorptive, adaptive, and transformative (Jeans et al., 2017; TANGO International, 2018).

Absorptive resilience is the ability to take preventive measures to decrease risk, impact, and exposure to hazards/disasters. The knowledge used in building absorptive resilience capacity is linked to technical (scientific) knowledge. For example, community members may implement mitigative measures based on information obtained from attending a disaster preparedness workshop or because of the information they may have received from reading a mitigation handbook (Jeans et al., 2017).

Adaptive resilience is the ability to make decisions based on lived experiences associated with social, economic, and environmental changes (Levine et al., 2011). The knowledge used in building adaptive resilience is linked to local (indigenous) knowledge, where a community person begins to take preparedness measures based on the ability to perceive climatic changes without the influence of technical knowledge (Levine et al., 2011). For instance, the ability of a farmer or a fisherman to recognize the change in cloud coverage, wind speed, or habitual behavior changes in the farm animals can predict an upcoming storm. With that prediction the local farmer or fisherman begins to take steps to reduce the risk of impact on his house.

Transformative resilience is the ability of the government to make systemic changes to protect constituents from hazards/disasters regardless of social and economic statuses (Pelling et al., 2014; Ziervogel et al., 2016). While in the past transformative resilience capacity was grounded in a utilitarian approach that solely relied on technical (scientific) knowledge, studies like that of Campbell and Marshall (2002) have shown that bringing multiple people to the table can help to design and implement better policies (Hudson et al., 1979). One example of this is the Louisiana Coastal Master Plan where planners, practitioners, and researchers allowed community members across the state of Louisiana to present a series of environmental problems resulting from human-made and natural hazards. While knowledge is only one part of increasing individual capacity to respond and recover from a disaster, it is an imperative first step that introduces practitioners, politicians, and researchers to the multiple needs that exist within the community.

In implementing the K.A.P.S. study, we found that many participants who had lived in the multi-hazard community of Geismar, Louisiana their entire lives initially lacked key preparedness technical knowledge that would decrease their susceptibility to a hazard (Semien and Nance, 2019). The results of the study also indicated participants possessed a level of adaptive capacity which enabled them to recognize a potential hazard and respond based on knowledge acquired through lived experiences. The results of the study indicated that there is a need to connect the gaps between technical knowledge and local knowledge to increase the resilience of those living within multi-hazard communities.

BOX 4.1 K.A.P.S. FEATURED COMMUNITY ACTIVIST 2
Sharon Lavigne
Founder, RISE St. James and Goldman Prize Winner

What are your primary focus areas in your community?

I am primarily focused on finding ways to stop the expansion of existing industries (chemical plants) in our parish and prevent industrial permitting for new petrochemical facilities. Our community is already filled with so many facilities and it does not need another one.

How did you get into this work and how long have you been in this work?

I am a retired teacher, but I have been involved in this work since 2018, when I first heard that Formosa Plastics, a $9.4 billion industry, would be coming into Saint James Parish. That's the spark that triggered me—I felt like God was leading me to do something ... so I did. I became involved with several other organizations, but none had the same mission I had which was to stop Formosa from moving into our community [St. James, Louisiana].

Do you think that your role as a teacher prepared you for what you're doing now as a community leader?

Yes, I feel like it goes hand in hand. In a way I am still teaching—providing information to the people of this community. So many people felt like they could not do anything until we started fighting. We challenged politicians who were part of the problem. We purchased billboards and flyers to bring awareness to the issue. Now those are expensive, but we were able to bring awareness to this issue.

Looking back, what do you wish you could have done differently?

I wish I would have reached out to the ministers first and let them reach out to their parishioners. I also wish I would have attended more classes and did more research so I could fully understand what this work entailed before starting.

How do you balance life and take care of yourself with the amount of work you take on?

- Workout
- Read Psalm 23
- Take time to do some things for myself
- Take a break on the weekends

  "When it's time for something [like a chemical plant] to come into [the community], don't leave it up to the politicians. Put it on the ballot. Let the citizens vote <u>for it</u> or <u>against it</u>. It's time for the citizens to speak up! It's time for a change!"

A (ATTITUDE) IN K.A.P.S.

While knowledge is a critical component of the K.A.P.S. model, knowledge cannot solely prepare an individual or a community for a disaster. Knowledge provides individuals with the information needed to make a decision. That decision is often influenced by lived experiences and social networks that affect an individual's attitudes, beliefs, and behavior. This next section examines the "A" for attitude in the K.A.P.S. model, providing methodologies to teach individuals how to make attitude adjustments, handle stress, and make appropriate decisions.

Types of Attitudes

Attitude can be defined as a mechanism in which an individual organizes their beliefs, feelings, and behavior with some degree of favor or disfavor (Hogg and Vaughan, 2005; Eagly and Chaiken, 1993). According to Ostrom (1969) there are three types of attitude structures also known as the ABC model.

1. *Affective*: the feelings and emotions that an individual exerts on an object and/or concept.
2. *Behavioral*: the activities and behavior that an individual exerts because of their feelings toward an object and/or concept.
3. *Cognitive*: what an individual thinks or perceives about an object and/or concept.

Each attitude structure offers a level of understanding as to why individuals maintain a certain attitude towards an object and/or concept. What a person believes to be true will influence their perception which can influence their willingness to mitigate, prepare, respond, and recover from a disaster (Ostrom, 1969; Ross, 1986; Basolo et al., 2009; Levac et al., 2012).

During a disaster, a person's ability to choose to mitigate, prepare, respond, and recover from a disaster lies heavily on their approach to the Affective, Behavioral, and Cognitive (ABC) model (Ostrom, 1969). For instance, a person who has a *positive behavioral attitude* will be willing to evacuate under a mandatory evacuation order posed by the local government, because they have a *positive cognitive attitude* that allows them to understand the need for evacuation. The contrary is also true if the individual has ill feelings and/or emotions toward the local government. These ill feelings may be the result of a *negative affective attitude* because of past experiences that contribute to their lack of trust for the government (Basolo et al., 2009). Another example may be that a person who has a *positive behavioral attitude* will be willing to properly mitigate their home and or gather preparedness supplies. This individual may have the *positive cognitive attitude* to understand the importance of performing these activities to protect their homes and their lives. While a person who has a *negative affective attitude* will typically refuse to mitigate their home and gather preparedness supplies. This may be because the individual feels that partaking in these activities is unnecessary based on their past experiences with storms.

The *negative affective attitudes* of an individual's social network can also influence an individual's negative behavioral attitudes, influencing them to not take mitigation or preparedness action. Minority individuals often rely heavily on social networks to obtain disaster-related information, like that of family, friends, churches, or social groups (McCoy and Dash, 2013; Bolin and Bolton, 1986; Chamlee-Wright and Storr, 2011), as compared to nationally validated sources like that of public officials or government organizations (McCoy and Dash, 2013; Bolin and Kurtz, 2017; Bolin and Bolton, 1986). This is often in relation to the inability of minority individuals to trust these sources of information, which in part may be due to previous social experiences with these institutions and/or people (Lindell, 2013; Perry, 1987; Berke et al., 2011). This is problematic because there is a high probability that the information that is received from social networks may be incomplete, inaccurate, or not up to date (McCoy and Dash, 2013; Lindell, 2013). This means that individuals are basing their attitudes on invalid information and may lack the willingness to mitigate/prepare for a disaster.

What Influences Attitudes

What a person perceives as true will influence their attitude and ultimately their decision to act (Basolo et al., 2009). That influence is often linked to three main stimuli: lived, learned, and accepted experiences (Zaman et al., 2020; Terpstra, 2011; Weber and Hsee, 1998). These three stimuli have a direct correlation on if/how an individual chooses to mitigate and prepare for a disaster (Bourque et al., 2013).

A person's *lived experience* of residing in a region that is highly elevated, not in a flood zone, and lacking man-made hazards will possess an attitude that will make them less likely to prepare for a disaster given a notice from officials. While another person's lived experience of residing in a region that is low in elevation, prone to floods and man-made hazards will possess an attitude that will make them more likely to prepare for a disaster given a notice from officials.

A person's *learned experience* derived from technical or scholarly information can have a direct impact on their ability to understand their risk, establish a positive attitude, and take appropriate steps to mitigate and/or prepare. While a person lacking learned experience may maintain a level of naiveness, creating a negative attitude that may prevent them from taking steps to mitigate and/or prepare.

A person's *accepted experiences* are those derived from other people's experience, this information is primarily shared through social networks and accepted based on conversations that occurred through those networks. A person who has a diverse social network who are well-educated in disasters will be exposed to a different level of information than those who are not connected to a diverse and well-educated social network.

Attitudes Impact on the Decision-Making Process

Theorists like Hanushek and Rivkin (1996) have predicted that as the benefit increases so will the choices made by individuals (Hanushek and Rivkin, 1996 as cited in Wallace and Wolf, 2006). As individuals we are constantly making calculated decisions based on lived, learned, and accepted experiences. Many of these calculated decisions are based on the ability to analyze the cost versus the benefit of taking part in an experience (Motoyshi, 2006). In relation to preparing, mitigating, or responding to a disaster an individual will only take part if he/she believes that the benefits outweigh the costs (Kousky et al., 2019). Ensuring that individuals understand that benefits outweigh the cost will allow individuals to develop a positive perception and take intended steps to proceed through the process effectively.

Offering rewards and/or incentives to help individuals proceed through the disaster cycle can help individuals make active decisions to prepare, mitigate, and respond. The more one is rewarded the more likely they are to keep progressing toward an intended goal and the more closely related the reward the more likely it is that an individual will perform well (Wallace and Wolf, 2006; Allmendinger, 2009). The work of Homans (1950) suggests that individuals respond to being rewarded and similar types of rewards (Wallace and Wolf, 2006; Allmendinger, 2009). However, the perceived value of the individual is lost when the same type of reward is received (Wallace and Wolf, 2006; Allmendinger, 2009). The more an individual values the process the more likely it is the individual will keep performing toward an intended goal, but individuals may become unhappy when their perception is not met with an expected reward (Wallace and Wolf, 2006; Allmendinger, 2009). Combining a reward as an added benefit will encourage individuals to proceed through the disaster cycle. If an individual does not feel that their benefits outweigh the cost, they will be less likely to mitigate and prepare for a disaster. Equipping the community with the knowledge and positive attitudes they need to prepare for a disaster is imperative and should be taught in culturally sustaining pedagogies with specific course objectives.

BOX 4.2 K.A.P.S. FEATURED PRACTITIONER SPOTLIGHT 2

Quianta Moore, M.D., J.D.
Founder, Catapult Dreams, LLC. Executive Director, The Hackett Center For Mental Health

What is your area of Specialty?

My area of specialty is early childhood development, and my work informs policy that will advance the physical and mental health of children.

How did you get into this work?

I am trained as both a medical doctor and a lawyer. In all honesty, my career really fell into my lap ... people thought I was a leader, so they placed me on advisory boards that helped cultivate my relationship with people in my field. From there, my interest in improving community health grew.

How does your work relate to disasters?

Children are often at risk for PTSD and child-abuse up to 6 months after a disaster. They are part of the vulnerable population and may need to be taught how to manage those traumas and emotions.

What strategy do you use to translate research into action for marginalized communities?

The biggest strategy I use to translate knowledge into action is to turn the science into simple language to increase understanding of content.

What do you wish you could have done differently now that you look back at your career?

My biggest mistake as a practitioner was thinking that I was always right when speaking with a community. I wish my initial approach was different because they are the expert in their communities. Now I know that humility today leads to curiosity tomorrow.

What is the biggest advice you have for other practitioners?

- Share resources
- Maintain integrity
- Develop and maintain relationships

What are some activities you use to "self-care?"

- Vacationing with my family
- Setting boundaries around the time I spend with my family

    "If I'm stressed out, I cannot be fully resilient and help those who need me—it's okay to take a break and recharge."

Learn more about Quianta Moore at https://mmhpi.org/staff/quianta-moore/

HOW DO WE TEACH IT?

The key to being an effective teacher is to ensure that students are able to meet course objectives while presenting the information in a manner that is relatable and applicable that embraces a culturally sustaining pedagogy. To ensure course objectives are defined and met, the K.A.P.S. Model followed a Bloom's Taxonomy framework for categorizing educational goals (Bloom, 1956). There are six components of the framework:

1. *Knowledge*: the ability to recall patterns, structures, and specifics.
2. *Comprehension*: the ability to understand and communicate information.

3. *Application*: the ability to employ what was learned in a real-life situation.
4. *Analysis*: the ability to breakdown information while clearly expressing the main ideas.
5. *Synthesis*: the ability to put together pieces of information to create an entire concept.
6. *Evaluation*: the ability to judge the quality and worth of the information presented.

Figure (4.2) shows how the K.A.P.S. Model integrates the six major concepts of Bloom's Taxonomy into the instructional material to ensure the information is relatable.

Bloom Taxonomy	Tools used in K.A.P.S. Workshop	Description of Usage in K.A.P.S. Workshop
Knowledge	• Imagery • Call and response	To influence individuals to recognize and recall previously presented information.
Comprehension	• Personalized material that summaries content	To provide participants with material to take home to share with families.
Application	• Skills building exercises	To encourage participants to execute, implement, differentiate, organize, and attribute newly acquired information.
Analysis	• Mid-session checkpoints • Group discussion	To encourage individuals to check and critique participants' understanding of the presented information.
Synthesis	• Skill building exercises • Problem-based exercises • Design preparedness plans and kits	To encourage participants to be creative in generating potential solutions to the problems given in the scenarios.
Evaluation	• Pre-test • Post-test	To measure the change in knowledge as a result of participating in the workshop.

FIGURE 4.2 Crosswalk between Bloom's Taxonomy of Educational Goals and the K.A.P.S. Framework

To ensure the information is relatable and applicable it is important to understand the audience and how they learn. According to the VARK Model produced by Fleming and Mills (1992), there are four learning styles that explain how one individual can take in information. Those learning styles are visual, auditory, reading/writing, and kinesthetic. See Figure (4.3) for a breakdown of the types of learners, definition, and the tools that can be used to increase learning among each group.

The K.A.P.S. Model is unique, as it develops instructional material that presents information that applies to all four learning styles to ensure that the information is relatable. For each section of the K.A.P.S. instructional period there was a designated activity that connected with one or more of the four types of learners. For instance, the first 10–15 minutes of the workshop was designed for the auditory learner as the instructor presented definitions and terminologies in a lecture format. The next 5 minutes of the workshop was designed for the reading/writing learner as the instructor encouraged the learner to complete worksheets and take notes on newly acquired information. The next 10–15 minutes of the workshop was designed for the kinesthetic learner as the instructor provided skill building activities through hands-on skill building

Type of Learner	Definition	K.A.P.S. Tools to Increase Learning
Visual learner	An individual who takes in information based on what they see.	• Graphics • Images • Diagrams • Symbols
Auditory learner	An individual who takes in information based on what they hear.	• Videos • Oral lectures • Written documents
Reading/writing learner	An individual who takes in information based on physically reading and writing information down for themselves.	• Physical hand-outs • Worksheets • Challenged to take detailed notes
Kinesthetic learner	An individual who takes in information based on what they feel with their hands.	• Hands-on interactive activities • Participatory presentations

FIGURE 4.3 Types of learning styles used in the K.A.P.S. Model

Source: Fleming and Mills (1992).

activity. Throughout the entire presentation we ensured that there were many images, graphics, and visual depictions of the information for the visual learner.

Using a Culturally Sustaining Pedagogy to Teach Disaster Preparedness

While there are many learning pedagogies that examine the theoretical and practical steps to learn and deliver information to students, the K.A.P.S. framework is grounded in culturally sustaining pedagogies. Culturally sustaining pedagogies "seek to perpetuate and foster—to sustain—linguistic, literate, and cultural pluralism as part of schooling for positive social transformation" (Paris and Alim, 2017: 1). In other words, it is the ability to sustain an individual's culture by embracing their language, literacies, histories, and culture (Paris and Alim, 2017).

Typically, training programs use a top-down approach where the trainer is the expert, and the trainee is the subordinate (Scott and Scott, 2016; Bowen and Marks, 1994). This is problematic because if left unchallenged this idea can leave community members delegitimized as they are being forced to assimilate to a system that fails to embrace all of their needs and cultural values (Paris and Alim, 2017). As an instructor it is important to approach students using a bottom-up approach that embodies their culture and builds trust. In doing so this will aid the instructor in navigating potential performance resistance behavior (Scott and Scott, 2016). Performance resistance is essentially a defense mechanism resulting from historic mistreatment and disenfranchisement. As an instructor the only way to eradicate this behavior is to approach participants in a manner that embraces their culture and teaches equity, while equipping them with the knowledge to resist misconceptions (Paris and Alim, 2017).

BOX 4.3 K.A.P.S. FEATURED MODEL 4

Lori Peek, Ph.D., Jennifer Tobin, Ph.D., Rachel M. Adams, Ph.D., Haorui Wu, Ph.D., Mason Clay Mathews, Ph.D.
Natural Hazards Center, University of Colorado Boulder

CONVERGE: A Framework for Convergence Research in the Hazards and Disaster Field

Model Definition

Convergence research is defined as an approach to knowledge production and action that involves diverse teams working together in novel ways—transcending disciplinary and organizational boundaries—to address vexing social, economic, environmental, and technical challenges in an effort to reduce disaster losses and promote collective well-being (Peek et al., 2020).

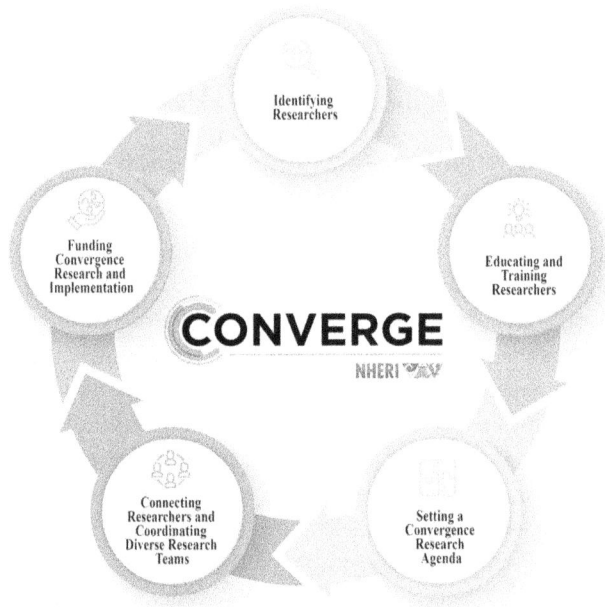

FIGURE 4.4 The Converge Model

Model Summary

The National Science Foundation-funded CONVERGE facility is dedicated to advancing ethically grounded convergence research in the hazards and disaster field. Convergence research requires interdisciplinary or even transdisciplinary

---

approaches. But it also goes beyond these approaches through offering a framework where members of the hazards and disaster research community come together to characterize the mounting threats communities face and, importantly, identify specific actions that will reduce the historical and socio-technical problems, inequalities, and injustices that turn natural hazards into disasters.

The CONVERGE facility, which is led by Dr. Lori Peek at the Natural Hazards Center at the University of Colorado Boulder, is the sole social-science-led facility in the broader Natural Hazards Engineering Research Infrastructure (NHERI) network for the United States. CONVERGE seeks to advance hazards and disaster research through building the social infrastructure to promote collaboration and convergence research. There are five main elements of the CONVERGE model:

- Identifying, educating, and training researchers;
- Setting a convergence research agenda that is problem-focused and solutions based;
- Connecting researchers and coordinating functionally and demographically diverse research teams;
- Supporting and funding convergence research, data collection, data sharing, and solutions implementations.

The work of CONVERGE and its partners is designed to democratize access to knowledge and ready researchers to both assess and address the many pressing social, economic, environmental, and technical challenges that lead to disaster losses.

Why Feature Convergence? Much like the K.A.P.S. Model, the CONVERGE model seeks to provide an inclusive as well as interdisciplinary approach to engage researchers, practitioners, and community members. The main idea behind both models is to produce research results that are more ethical, problem-focused, and solutions-oriented.

Learn more about the CONVERGE model at: Peek, L., Tobin, J., Adams, R. M., Wu, H., & Mathews, M. C. (2020). A framework for convergence research in the hazards and disaster field: The Natural Hazards Engineering Research Infrastructure CONVERGE facility. Frontiers in Built Environment, 6, 110. https://www.frontiersin.org/articles/10.3389/fbuil.2020.00110/full
Visit the Converge site: https://converge.colorado.edu/.

WHAT DO WE TEACH?

The K.A.P.S. Model followed the Krathwohl (2002) method for delivering knowledge which states that there are four types of knowledge: (1) factual, (2) conceptual, (3) procedural, and (4) metacognitive knowledge.

Factual knowledge is the information needed to fully understand a discipline (Krathwohl, 2002). This type of knowledge often includes definition, terminologies,

K.A.P.S	Term	Definition	Source
Knowledge	**Knowledge**	The facts, information, and skills acquired by a person through experience or education.	Dewey (1989)
	Hazard	A natural or anthropogenic threat (i.e. earthquake, tornado, flood, chemical spill, explosion, fire).	Perry (2007)
	Disaster	Quick onset of events with significant impacts from the natural environment upon the socioeconomic system.	Alexander (1993) in Perry (2007)
	Vulnerability	Susceptibility or potential for experiencing the harmful impacts of a hazard event.	
	Social Vulnerability	The characteristics of a person or group in terms of their capacity to anticipate, cope with, resist and recover from the impacts of a natural hazard.	Blaikie et al. (1994)
	Hurricane	A type of storm called a tropical cyclone, which forms over tropical or subtropical waters. Hurricanes are rated on a Saffir-Simpson Hurricane Wind Scale and given a rating of 1 to 5.	NOAA (2013)
	Tornado	A tornado is a narrow, violently rotating column of air that extends from the base of a thunderstorm to the ground.	NOAA (2013)
	Flooding	An overflowing of water onto land that is normally dry.	NOAA (2013)
Attitude	**Attitude**	A relatively enduring organization of beliefs, feelings, and behavioral tendencies towards socially significant objects, groups, events or symbols.	Hogg and Vaughan (2005)
	React	Failure of an individual to stop and process information before taking steps.	K.A.P.S.
	Respond	The ability to stop and process information prior to taking steps.	K.A.P.S.
Preparedness	**Disaster Preparedness**	Measures taken to reduce the effects of disasters. That is, to predict and, where possible, prevent disasters, mitigate their impact on vulnerable populations.	IFRC (2021)
	Sheltering in Place	Finding a safe location indoors and staying there until you are given an "all clear" or told to evacuate.	Yale (n.d.)
	Natural Disaster	Includes all types of severe weather, which have the potential to pose a significant threat to human health and safety, property, critical infrastructure, and homeland security.	DHS (2021)
	Man-made Disaster	Man-made disasters are extreme hazardous events that are caused by human beings. Some examples of man-made disaster emergencies include chemical spills, hazardous material spills, explosions, chemical or biological attacks, nuclear blasts, train accidents, plane crashes, or groundwater contamination.	NEHA (2021)
Skill	**Skill**	A set of physical activities that enable an individual to respond appropriately and effectively to a disaster.	K.A.P.S.
	Disaster Preparedness Plan	Identifying organizational resources, determining roles and responsibilities, developing policies and procedures and planning activities in order to reach a level of preparedness to be able to respond timely and effectively to a disaster should one occur.	IFRC (2021)
	Disaster Preparedness Kit	Disaster supplies kit includes food, clothing, first aid supplies, tools, and key documents.	Sutton and Tierney (2006)

FIGURE 4.5 Terms and definitions of the K.A.P.S. Model

specific details, and elements (Krathwohl, 2002). See Figure 4.5 for a brief list of terms and definitions that the K.A.P.S. training included in their workshop.

Conceptual knowledge is the relationship that exists between all acquired information and the components which enables them to work together to produce a broader understanding of a concept (Krathwohl, 2002). This type of knowledge often includes classifications, categories, principles, generalizations, theoretical models, and structures (Krathwohl, 2002). See Figure 4.6 for an example model depicting hurricane classification that the K.A.P.S. training included in their workshop.

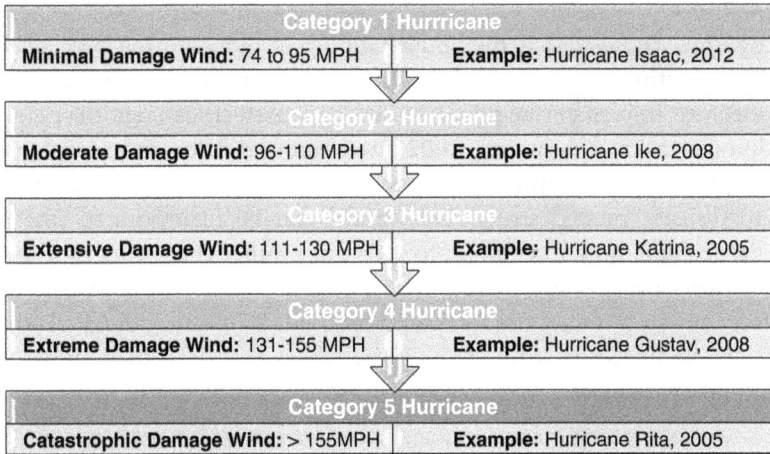

Category 1 Hurrricane	
Minimal Damage Wind: 74 to 95 MPH	**Example:** Hurricane Isaac, 2012

Category 2 Hurricane	
Moderate Damage Wind: 96-110 MPH	**Example:** Hurricane Ike, 2008

Category 3 Hurricane	
Extensive Damage Wind: 111-130 MPH	**Example:** Hurricane Katrina, 2005

Category 4 Hurricane	
Extreme Damage Wind: 131-155 MPH	**Example:** Hurricane Gustav, 2008

Category 5 Hurricane	
Catastrophic Damage Wind: > 155MPH	**Example:** Hurricane Rita, 2005

FIGURE 4.6 Hurricane categories and descriptions

Procedural knowledge is knowledge of how to implement acquired knowledge (Krathwohl, 2002). This type of knowledge often includes skills, techniques, methods, and criteria for implementing procedures. See Figure 4.7 for an example model that points out step-by-step how to make a disaster preparedness plan.

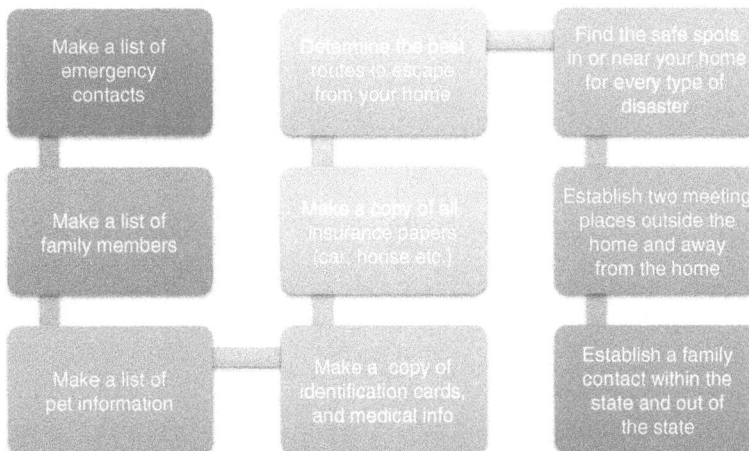

Make a list of emergency contacts

Determine the best routes to escape from your home

Find the safe spots in or near your home for every type of disaster

Make a list of family members

Make a copy of all insurance papers (car, house etc.)

Establish two meeting places outside the home and away from the home

Make a list of pet information

Make a copy of identification cards, and medical info

Establish a family contact within the state and out of the state

FIGURE 4.7 Step-by-step procedure for making a disaster preparedness plan

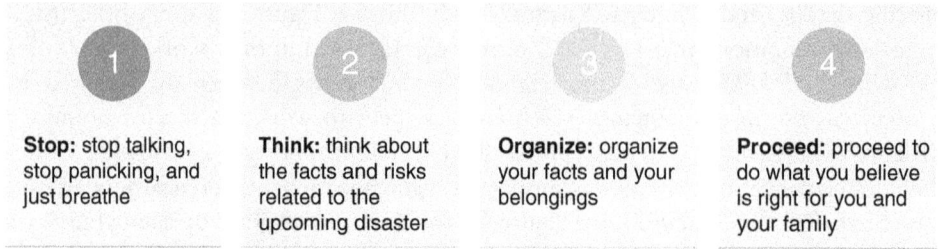

Stop: stop talking, stop panicking, and just breathe

Think: think about the facts and risks related to the upcoming disaster

Organize: organize your facts and your belongings

Proceed: proceed to do what you believe is right for you and your family

FIGURE 4.8 Step-by-step procedure for regulating stress

Metacognitive knowledge is the understanding of our own self-perceptions, reasoning, and intuition (Krathwohl, 2002). This type of knowledge often includes strategic steps to implement acquired knowledge, as well as cognitive, contextual, and conditional tasks (Krathwohl, 2002). See Figure 4.8 for an example model to help participants with a step-by-step procedure of how to encourage members to respond to disaster related stress. This model can be incorporated into training to teach participants how to *respond* to a disaster rather than *react* to a disaster to prevent bad decision making (Prezenski et al., 2017). When an individual *responds* to a disaster they stop, think, organize, and proceed. While an individual who *reacts* to a disaster just proceeds without thinking, which may lead to multiple levels of stress and unpreparedness.

CHAPTER 5

Applying the Preparedness and Skills in K.A.P.S.

....

The next two components of the K.A.P.S. Model are "P" for preparedness and "S" for skills. The physical aspects of preparedness are imperative to ensure a community is equipped to handle a disaster, while skills are the techniques and methodologies needed to implement preparedness.

This chapter focuses on applying the preparedness and skills in K.A.P.S. within communities by (1) unpacking what it means to be prepared for a disaster, (2) presenting specific methodologies for addressing disasters, (3) providing concepts that should be taught within instructional workshops, and (3) providing methods to teach preparedness and skills. Like Chapter 4, this chapter also includes a sample lesson plan for teaching preparedness and skills application using the K.A.P.S. Model and is inclusive of the exact lesson plans used in implementing the original K.A.P.S. workshop.

P (PREPAREDNESS) IN K.A.P.S.

The emergency management cycle or disaster cycle that is widely accepted by disaster researchers consist of four stages: mitigation, preparedness, response, and recovery. While it is preferred that communities begin the cycle at the preparedness and mitigation stages, many communities do not approach the cycle until after a disaster, in the response and recovery phases (Lindell, 2013; Perry, 1987). This may be for a variety of reasons such as risk perception, physical ability to access resources as well as social acceptability to participate in the cycle within its early stages (Bourque et al., 2013; Lindell, 2013).

While each stage is a critical component worth studying, this book primarily addresses the preparedness stage. The preparedness stage of the disaster cycle is critical to reduce fatalities, injuries, and economic losses that may be the result of natural and anthropogenic origins (Look and Spennemann, 2001). The key to deescalating the next

DOI: 10.4324/9781003177005-7

disaster is for individual households to be adequately prepared for the occurrence of a disaster by tapping into resources geared toward disaster preparedness education and empowerment (Karanci et al., 2005).

Disaster Preparedness Education and Empowerment

Educating and empowering the community to be prepared is critical to reduce their risk of exposure and impact from a hazard. Through education community members can learn lifesaving skills that can be applied if a disaster occurs (Hoffman and Muttarak, 2017). These measures can include information on decision making needed to shelter in place and/or evacuate given the onset of a hazard event (McEntire, 2015). Life-sustaining measures can also be acquired through disaster education where community members can learn how to obtain key survival resources like what items should and should not be stockpiled prior to a hazard event (i.e., water, batteries, important paperwork, matches, non-perishable food items) (Sutton and Tierney, 2006). Given successful execution preparedness measures can also reduce the number of structural damages acquired because of a disaster (McEntire, 2015; Khan, 2008).

During a disaster there is always urgency for resources from the government, yet the availability of those resources is often limited, and the response times are often extremely slow due to bureaucratic regulations (Paton and Johnston, 2001). Overestimating the government resources and response times can lead to limited participation under the assumption that the government will appear on the scene in a timely manner with an abundance of resources (Wingate et al., 2007; Paton and Johnston, 2001). This is often not the case making it imperative that all community members are equipped with the knowledge and skills to respond appropriately to various hazards. Through empowerment, community members can learn how to think critically as well as respond appropriately without relying heavily on social networks or government assistance (Zimmerman, 2000; Perkins and Zimmerman, 1995; Paton, 2003).

Disaster Preparation Challenges

Marginalized communities are often excluded when cities develop strategies to plan and prepare for a disaster (Finch et al., 2010). Communities that are of lower income and minority are often last to hear about public informationals and trainings that provide relevant information about evacuation routes, disaster kits (i.e., flashlights, batteries etc.) and other preparedness strategies (Morrow, 1999). To ensure residents are well prepared for a disaster, the local government should follow up with residents to ensure they have extra supplies and know how to access resources prior to a disaster (i.e., distributing evacuation routes and location of open shelters).

Vulnerable populations within marginalized communities are often the individuals who are least likely to be prepared for a disaster and the most at risk to a hazard (Lippmann, 2011; Moore et al., 2004). These vulnerable groups often include children, elderly, disabled, single-headed households, illiterate, low income, and minorities (Thomas et al., 2013). Contributing factors that can inhibit preparedness levels among vulnerable groups can include but are not limited to lack of financial re-sources, time, accessibility, and knowledge (Peacock et al., 2012; Laska and Morrow, 2006).

FIGURE 5.1 Homes in Narco, Louisiana near a chemical plant

For instance, individuals who live on a limited income often lack the extra money needed to stockpile resources (Pastor et al., 2006; Bullard and Wright, 2009). The working class does not have the time to collect the supplies needed to prepare for a possible disaster or even the space in their home to keep the extra supplies (McCoy and Dash, 2013). A working-class single parent may lack the time to attend known preparatory workshops, preventing them from acquiring critical information needed to prepare their household (Lippmann, 2011; Moore et al., 2004). An elderly or disabled person may also lack the ability to purchase needed preparedness supplies due to lack of fiscal resources (Peek, 2013). They may not be able to physically attend a workshop or have access to the internet, preventing them from obtaining preparedness information.

Communication as a Link to Community Preparedness

Although preparedness is one method to build resources and take measures to reduce the impact of a disaster, if the information is not adequately communicated and practiced, the success rates will be extremely low (Eisenman et al., 2007). Take for example, the aftermath of the 2005 Hurricane Katrina occurrence in New Orleans, Louisiana. A study completed by Wingate in 2007 showed that 75 percent of the deaths occurring during Hurricane Katrina were among the elderly, representing 15 percent of the city's population (Wingate et al., 2007). In addition, Wingate et al. stated that "nearly all of the 280 nursing homes in New Orleans remained full despite the calls for evacuation … resulting in the death of over 200 residents" (2007: 422). After examining the evacuation plans associated with these nursing homes, Wingate and colleagues found that the nursing homes made plans to have residents evacuate via school buses but due to technicalities in the execution of the plan there was no one there to drive those school buses. As a result, much of the city's elderly population lost their lives due to the poor execution of disaster plans. When vulnerable populations are not clearly identified with clear and practiced executable plans, the results are catastrophic.

Having a plan is one thing but being able to use the plan is a completely different task (Banks, 2013). One of the greatest ways to ensure community preparedness is to actively involve the community through "public and private partnerships" (Sutton and Tierney, 2006; Banks, 2013). Developing partnerships with community members creates space to share and distribute information. Every individual and family within a community plays a role in developing effective tools that can prevent future casualties. However, no one individual or family can act completely independently (Suda, 2000; Banks, 2013). Partnerships should focus on preparing both the individuals and the community for the possibility of a disaster to prevent or reduce future casualties (Look and Spennemann, 2001).

BOX 5.1 K.A.P.S. FEATURED PRACTITIONER SPOTLIGHT 3

Alessandra Jerolleman, Ph.D.
Allesandra Jerolleman, LLC

What is your area of specialty?

I would say my area of specialty is disaster recovery, climate mitigation, climate adaptation, and hazard mitigation. I focus on justice and equity framed in applied and participatory planning.

How did you get into this work?

I have been working in this field for about 16 years. I initially became involved in this work while working in an applied Research Center at the University of New Orleans with Shirley Laska and Kristina Peterson, who are now cofounders of the Lowlander Center.

How have you addressed the problems of participatory planning and disaster research from marginalized communities in your career?

One of the things that has been important for me is to have the community leaders not just as partners in the research, but leaders in the research. The community needs to have a voice in deciding what research needs to be done. I don't believe that we have the right to treat other people as subjects and not as equal partners. I don't think intellectual curiosity justifies putting any community in the Petri dish, I can't imagine doing research any other way than framed ethically and value laden.

Have you faced any challenges in your work in getting partnerships and building trust?

While many of my relationships grew out of the work I was doing with other partners, it still took me a long time to build trust within the community. I think one of the challenges that I have had is deciding how much of my own voice to use, especially when the research is intended to be led by the community. On one hand sometimes I have an outsider perspective on some of the pitfalls and the downsides to some of the decisions that the community might make, but it's still their decision to make and I am here to support them through that process.

What do you wish you could have done differently now that you look back at your career?

I wish I would have taken the time to have stronger relationships because they make a difference. It's important to be intentional and have an open mind when working with marginalized communities.

What are some best practices and ways of how you've navigated those situations?

- Encourage the community to obtain copyrights and ownership over their work as well as their ideas.
- Check your intentions and make sure you have an entirely open mind.
- Be patient and let go of your ego – be prepared to be called out for things you didn't do. You will be inheriting the baggage of every other interaction that the community has had before with practitioners and scholars alike.
- Remember you are just one piece of a bigger puzzle.

"The cost of a failure is utterly different for the researcher who can step away at the end of the day. We're talking about people's lives and livelihoods."

Learn more about Alessandra Jerolleman: http://alessandrajerolleman.com/

S (SKILLS) IN K.A.P.S.

Being prepared stretches well beyond common disaster knowledge and encompasses the actual skills needed to be successful. To develop those skills needed to be adequately prepared for a disaster, individuals, families, business, and communities must practice techniques to deal with pre- and post-disaster impacts. In the event of a disaster occurrence, people may have the resources to effectively deal with the issues at hand but lack the skills needed for execution (Wingate et al., 2007). Deaths and disasters can be reduced if individuals are thoroughly prepared by developing a plan, having a disaster preparedness kit, and practicing what is in the plan (Thomas et al., 2015; Kim and Zakour, 2017).

Types of Skills

While there is a plethora of skills that can be unpacked and utilized in ensuring that community members are well equipped for a disaster, a study performed by Wade et al., (2014) provides five types of skills for assisting the community with coping with a disaster. The skills are:

1. Building problem solving skills
2. Promoting positive activities
3. Managing reactions
4. Promoting helpful thinking
5. Rebuilding healthy social connections

Problem solving skills primarily focus on recognizing a problem and strategically planning to address that problem (Wade et al., 2014). In preparing for a disaster, this skill set creates space for individuals to think critically about how to prepare for a disaster and how to respond appropriately (Thomas et al., 2015; Kapucu, 2008). Decisions that may need critical thought may include the deciding between sheltering in place or evacuating (Haynes et al., 2009; Mannan and Kilpatrick, 2000). For instance, a family that is of low income and lives in an older, subpar home that is in a flood zone may lack the fiscal and physical resources needed to evacuate a community that is at risk from a disaster. This family has two choices: either do nothing and bear the consequences or think critically and reduce their risk from a disaster. Thinking critically for this family may be for the head of the household to go to the local lumber yard and ask for reduced or free wood to board up the windows of their home to prevent damages. The head of the household could also contact the city/county office to obtain free sandbags to prevent water from entering their home. The decision may also include deciding whether to evacuate to a local shelter or deciding to shelter in place. If deciding to shelter in place, the head of the household could also reach out to the local food pantry or nonprofit to obtain non-perishable food. See Figures 5.2 and 5.3 for images depicting an American Red Cross distribution site that offered supplies and resources to the community after the 2016 Baton Rouge, Louisiana flooding.

Promoting positive activities focuses on implementing the strategic plan (Wade et al., 2014). In disaster preparation it's the ability to follow the steps outlined in a preparedness, mitigation, or evacuation plan without having a melt-down during the onset of a disaster. Mitigation, preparedness, and evacuation plans are critical for survival given a disaster onset (Levac et al., 2012; Kapucu, 2008). The plans should discuss key mitigation strategies that an individual/family will use to handle a future disaster. These tactics should include "building a disaster supply kit... [outlining] specific protective actions to take, and property protection measures" (Sutton and Tierney, 2006: 15). Each plan should focus on the execution of every dimension of

FIGURE 5.2 The American Red Cross distribution site in Baton Rouge, Louisiana, held during "The Great Flood" of 2016

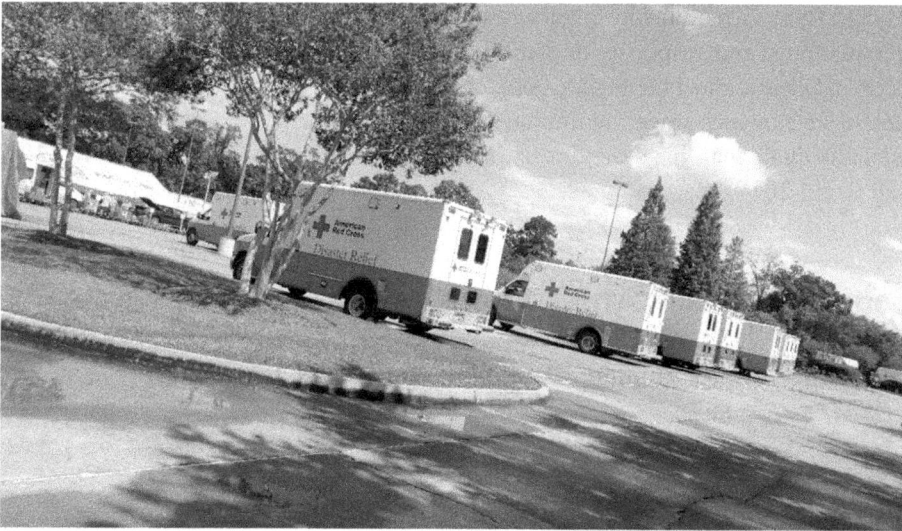

FIGURE 5.3 The American Red Cross distribution site in Baton Rouge, Louisiana, held during "The Great Flood" of 2016

disaster mitigation, preparedness, response, and recovery. The plans should not be arbitrary but should be family specific with key information that will help a family safely shelter in place or evacuate (Becker et al., 2012).

Managing reactions is the ability to control psychological triggers that may inadvertently lead to panic (Wade et al., 2014). This skill can also be coupled with *promoting helpful thinking* which is the ability to control negative thoughts and communications that would also inadvertently lead to panic (Wade et al., 2014). While we covered both skills in Chapter 4, this combined behavioral skill set can be defined as the decision to *react* or *respond* during a stressful situation. In Chapter 4 we described the decision to *react* as a failure of an individual to stop and process information before taking steps, while the decision to *respond* can be described as the ability to stop and process information prior to taking steps. Deciding whether to *react* or *respond* can play a contributing factor in decreasing stress levels among individuals during a disaster and can also help an individual successfully process information before making a major decision that may have an impact on their ultimate survival post impact (Joseph et al., 1993).

Finally, *rebuilding healthy social connections* focuses on building strong social networks prior to a disaster that can be used to support disaster mitigation, preparedness, response, and recovery. In minority and low-income communities, individuals rely heavily on social capital in the form of social networks to obtain information on which to base their decisions. Social capital is often referred to as the "glue" that causes individuals to become bonded, bridged, or linked to each other (Beaulieu, 2014; Nakagawa and Shaw, 2004; Brett and Oviatt, 2013). These networks bring individuals together, creating larger groups that build trust and provide greater access to resources (Bolin and Bolton, 1986; Chamlee-Wright and Storr, 2011). "There is perhaps no area where relationships are more critical than in disaster planning and response, and these relationships must be built before disaster strikes" (Gibson and Hayunga, 2006: 7). Building these connections prior to a disaster strike can encourage the mutual exchange of information, as well as resources that individuals may have previously lacked access to (Nakagawa and Shaw, 2004; Xiao et al., 2018).

BOX 5.2 K.A.P.S. FEATURED MODEL 5

A Framework for Democratization of Geospatial Technology
David Padgett, Ph.D.
Founder, Geomental Consulting

Model Definition

A method for EMPOWERING communities using geospatial technology. The model's goal is to EMPOWER communities in such a way that the individuals are equipped and independent to use geospatial skills, tools, and resources.

Model Summary

This form of participatory mapping among environmental justice communities provides an opportunity to democratize geospatial technologies and empower the communities to use this technology on their own. While there are many technologies (e.g., EJ Screen) available to marginalized communities to map their environmental justice challenges, the technology often goes unused. Geotechnologies often have somewhat of a steep learning curve and those living in marginalized communities are often untrained and unskilled in these technologies, making it incredibly difficult to use the available tools.

This model makes Geotechnologies available and useful to communities that are engaging in environmental justice activism by producing a twofold positive effect. First, the model connects the more mature activists with younger generations building relationships and "hopefully" increasing the interest of young people towards the field Geotechnologies. Younger people are often more adept to the technologies making it easier to produce swift and high-quality results. Second, the model provides the mature activists with a visual display of the problems that exist within the community.

While Geotechnologies may be daunting for those who are not adept, participatory mapping can play a significant role in advocating for environmental justice communities. Developing interactive maps can help activists portray disparities like food insecurities, industrial pollutants, and lack of available evacuation shelters in a marginalized community. The reality is that there are some things that cannot be seen until you place them on a map and overlay sociodemographic layers. The layering of information provides advocates with a visual depiction of the challenges the community faces. The more we empower these communities the better they are equipped to fight their own battles using their own voices.

Why Feature Geospatial Technology?

The model on Democratization of Geospatial Technology is novel in its approach to increase the capacity of marginalized groups to visually and independently depict their community challenges. This model's mission is similar to the mission of the K.A.P.S. Model to increase the knowledge, attitudes, preparedness and skills of communities in a way that allows the disenfranchised to identify their own challenges and effectively advocate on their own behalf.

> **Learn more about Dr. Padgett and the Democratization of Geospatial Technology:** American Geographical Society (AGS) Ethical-GEO Fellows Project. https://ethicalgeo.org/david-padgett-2/

HOW DO WE TEACH IT?

In the past, trainings have been taught with a traditional lecture from a top-down approach where the trainer supplies high quality information, and the trainee receives the information. The problem with this method is that these workshops are often culturally insensitive, socially, and culturally un-relatable. In some cases, the information distributed is taught at a high scholarly level that may not be received well by individuals with a lower education level (Fothergill and Peek, 2004). As a result, the information and resources supplied may go unheeded. To increase receptibility, retention, and application among individuals it is important to teach from a culturally sensitive, relatable constructivist approach (Gundlach and McDonough, 2011).

Ernest von Glasersfeld, an Asturian philosopher best known for radical constructivism, believed that "knowledge is not passively received but actively built up by the cognizing subject" (Von Glasersfeld, 1989). Through his theory he helped instructors move from a traditional lecture-based method of instruction to a hands-on problem-solving based instructional method (Hung et al., 2008; Wood, 2003). Von Glasersfeld believed that to obtain knowledge students should be placed in small groups and given real-life exercises to solve to ensure information was retained and students were able to critically apply that information. In working with historically marginalized groups (i.e., low income, minorities, female-headed households, elderly, disabled, etc.) it is important to go over and beyond to ensure that individuals are able to recall and apply information.

While some may believe that learning is just obtaining knowledge, scholars like Bronfenbrenner (1977) believe that learning is an active experience that is socially and culturally rooted. While in Chapter 4 we unpacked the types of learners, we would be amiss if we failed to address how sociodemographics, socioeconomics, culture, and environment relate to how individuals learn. The Bronfenbrenner ecological framework of human development supplies a theoretical approach to understand this relationship (Crawford et al., 2020; Bronfenbrenner and Morris, 1998). The model suggests that there are five categories that directly impact an individual's development: microsystem, mesosystem, exosystem, macrosystem, and chronosystem. Each system has relationships that are both indirectly and directly related that can impact whether an individual decides to evacuate or shelter in place.

The *microsystem* comprises groups of people that have a direct impact on the development, this may include bosses, coworkers, relatives, friends, and other community members (Bronfenbrenner, 1977; Bronfenbrenner and Morris, 1998; Bronfenbrenner, 1995). In terms of disaster research, the microsystem can have a direct impact on an individual's decision to evacuate or stay at home. As an instructor developing a training course it is important to include exercises and conversations that relate to the microsystems of an individual. The lesson plan could include skill building exercises that provide examples of both encouraging social networks and non-encouraging social networks.

BOX 5.3 MICROSYSTEM EXAMPLE

If *Individual A* asks *Coworker A* for advice for an upcoming storm who has never directly experienced a disaster, *Coworker A* may tell *Individual A* not to prepare for a disaster because they have never directly experienced a disaster themselves. The contrary is also true, if *Individual A* asks *Coworker B* for advice on an upcoming storm and *Coworker B* has firsthand experienced with a disaster than *Coworker B* will be able to tell *Individual A* how to prepare and respond to an upcoming storm.

Next is the *mesosystem* which is comprised of the interrelations that groups from the *microsystem* may have with each other (Bronfenbrenner, 1977; Bronfenbrenner and Morris, 1998; Bronfenbrenner, 1995). In terms of disaster research, the mesosystem may be influenced by the linkage that the *Individual A* family member may have with a friend of *Individual A*. As an instructor developing a training course, it is important to include exercises and conversations that relate to the mesosystems of an individual. For instance, the lesson plan could include skill building exercises that provide examples of the interrelations of groups from the microsystem.

BOX 5.4 MESOSYSTEM EXAMPLE

If *Individual A* approaches a family member who is a native resident of a community that does not regularly flood for advice and a friend who is native to the area, both parties may advise *Individual A* that there is no need to prepare or respond to an upcoming storm. While the contrary is also true, if *Individual A* approaches a family member who is a native resident of a community that regularly floods for advice and a friend who is native to the area, both parties may recommend that *Individual A* evacuate as the upcoming storm may cause a great level of impact in the region. The advice received from both parties may offer a great amount of weight in *Individual A's* role in deciding to either shelter in place or evacuate given an upcoming storm.

Next is the *exosystem* which is the link between social environments that do not directly involve an individual (Bronfenbrenner, 1977; Bronfenbrenner and Morris, 1998; Bronfenbrenner, 1995). As an instructor including exercises and conversations that relate to the ecosystems of an individual is imperative to help individuals make credible decisions regardless of their social environments.

BOX 5.5 EXOSYSTEM EXAMPLE

Consider a two-parent working household that becomes a one parent working divorced household. In this case the children are forced to adapt to a new social environment that consists of living with the one-parent divorcee. The above example relates to disaster research because one-parent households often experience a greater level of care-giving responsibility, making it incredibly difficult to prepare and respond for a disaster. Failure to prepare as well as respond either physically or fiscally could result in a greater level of damages creating a negative social environment for the children in the home.

Next the *Macrosystem* is the area that deals directly with cultural influences which can differ based on heritage, values, geographic regions, and sociodemographic and socioeconomic differences (Bronfenbrenner, 1977; Bronfenbrenner and Morris, 1998; Bronfenbrenner, 1995). These differences can play a heavy role in influencing an individual to prepare for and respond to the possibility of a disaster onset. As an instructor, including examples of culture, heritage, and values relative to the community in the lesson plans can help the lesson be more relatable and offer a sense of validation to the presented content.

BOX 5.6 MACROSYSTEM EXAMPLE

For instance, *Individual A* may live on land that has been in his/her family for generations, they are asked to evacuate, they may decline because they believe they need to be on the property to protect it from damages.

Another example of cultural influences is *Individual B* who may have strong inferences that if a disaster happens it is "an act of God's"—they may believe that if damages or death occurs it is God's will—as a result they may not prepare or respond in the interest of self-preparedness.

The last pattern is the *Chronosystem* which is used to describe the continuous patterns of events (Bronfenbrenner, 1977; Bronfenbrenner and Morris, 1998; Bronfenbrenner, 1995). In disaster research, patterns of disaster onset are typically prevalent among marginalized communities (Lippman, 2011). As an instructor, including case studies of the chronosystems that directly make up the community can offer individuals support in understanding the risks as well as the available mitigation strategies that can help prevent or reduce those impacts.

BOX 5.7 CHRONOSYSTEM EXAMPLE

Typically, marginalized communities are in low-lying areas, have poor infrastructure, are low income, and lack resources. As a result, the individuals living in the community may not be able to evacuate, and may be regularly exposed to environmental (i.e., hurricanes, tornadoes, wildfires, flooding) and anthropogenic (i.e., chemical spills, industrial explosions, oil spills, natural gas leaks) impacts. These impacts may occur in a pattern where every few years a similar event occurs, and the community members learn to adapt as they are continuously exposed to hazardous events.

The uniqueness of Bronfenbrenner's ecological systems theory is that it enables an instructor to understand the influences that external factors may have on the individual's ability to learn (Bronfenbrenner, 1974, 1977, 1995, 2000). In understanding these five systems, an instructor can now create a safe space where students can provide self-expression, pose questions, listen, and engage with both the instructor as well as other students in the class. Learned information should equip individuals to critically assess their own individual experiences, filter out other individuals' experiences, and enable them to apply key objectives that will increase their ability to proceed through the entire disaster cycle.

WHAT DO WE TEACH?

In designing and implementing a K.A.P.S. training program it was important for us to ensure participants could assess their risk and recall the skills needed to respond to the onset of a disaster. The K.A.P.S. workshop included hazard scenarios, and problem solving that allowed individuals to develop the critical thinking skills needed to address challenges that may arise during a storm (Semien and Nance, 2019; Albanese and Mitchell, 1993). We expanded beyond the distribution of resources and included empowerment exercises that both increased knowledge while also ensuring individuals were able to recall and apply information (Sutton and Tierney, 2006). These empowerment exercises embodied the theoretical approaches of constructivism (hands-on) and problem-based learning (Savery, 2015; Finucane et al., 1998).

Constructivism theory is the assumption that all learning is derived from either active or social experiences (Arends, 1998). Constructivism is "an approach to learning that holds that people actively construct or make their own knowledge and that reality is determined by the experiences of the learner" (Elliott et al., 2000: 256). It is the link between what an individual has already experienced in life combined with the ability to learn new information in a manner that is fully hands-on (Arends, 1998). In developing a disaster training it is imperative that the instructor develops exercises that asks participants to recall past experiences to unpack successes and mistakes. In some cases, exercises may be emotionally triggering so it is also important that the instructor is equipped to manage these challenges or can point the individual to a mental health specialist to help reduce their emotional dismay.

Problem Based Learning

Problem based learning is another theoretical teaching method that will allow an instructor to use real-world problems to encourage critical thinking among participants.

According to Duch et al. (2001) the most effective problem-based learning exercises should be those that motivate individuals to acquire a deeper level of understanding and make decisions based on reason rather than emotions. These scholars also suggested that the exercises should be well connected to course objectives, are complex, open-ended, and engaging (Duch et al., 2001). The major idea of problem-based learning is to ensure that an individual can absorb a set of complex information and then apply critical thinking skills to use that information to solve a real-world problem.

In developing the K.A.P.S. Model we combined Bronfenbrenner's ecological systems theory, Constructivism theory, and problem-based learning theory to ensure that the information acquired through the training was relatable as well as applicable given an onset of a disaster. Many of the exercises included recall behaviors that consisted of hazard scenarios, problem solving to reduce community vulnerability, and reduce potential challenges that may arise during a storm (Paton and Johnston, 2001). In the lesson plans we focused our trainings on hurricanes, chemical emergencies, tornadoes, and flooding. Each section provided a definition of what to do if one of these hazards were at risk to directly impacting a community offering a brief overview of how to evacuate and shelter in place. In addition, each section also offered mitigation strategies that highlighted communication strategies with key members of an individual's social network. Finally, each section also highlights the need for a system of checks and balances that individuals to keep track of all the members of their social networks while ensuring that their direct family members have reached safety.

BOX 5.8 K.A.P.S. FEATURED MODEL 6

A Framework for Preservation
Kathe Hambrick
Founder, River Road African American Museum

Model Definition

To educate visitors about the history and culture of African Americans in the rural communities of South Louisiana through the collection, preservation, and interpretation of art, artifacts, and historic buildings.

Model Summary

The River Road African American Museum is more than a History Museum and an Art Museum it's a place of both transformation and preservation that seeks to empower the next generation. Our mission is to preserve history in such a way that encourages, empowers, and drives change through preservation. The reality is that we are part of a village, and the story of that village is worth preserving for the future.

As a museum located in South Louisiana, we are often directly and indirectly challenged with the possibility of a disaster. This reality often challenges us to ask the question "how is the next disaster going to impact history and how we record history." As a preservationist at the museum, it's important that we consistently document oral history through video before and after a disaster so that we can capture the untold stories and experiences of those living within impacted communities. During Hurricane Katrina the museum's knowledge of *Benevolent Societies* helped to establish an organization called "The True Friends of the Flood." The organization collected oral histories as well as fiscal resources to be distributed in the form of gas cards and pharmacy cards to those affected by Hurricane Katrina.

In South Louisiana industries are another challenge preservationists are faced with as these institutions are consistently coming into the area and changing the landscapes. Without consistently documenting the oral histories as well as the artifacts, the knowledge and experiences would be forever lost, leaving the histories of communities to be told by those who never stepped foot into the community. The River Road African American Museum is more than just a typical museum, it is an institution that embodies freedom, resilience, and reconciliation.

Why Feature the River Road African American Museum?

True empowerment is linked to knowledge—the more knowledge a person has enables them to critically assess the challenges they are faced with daily. Preservation supplies the link between the knowledge of the past and the knowledge of the future. Like the K.A.P.S. Model, the museum seeks to build knowledge and awareness to empower individuals to increase their long-term capacities.

Learn more about the River Road African American Museum at: https://africanamericanmuseum.org/

PART III

Implementing K.A.P.S.

....

Given the limited number of academic researchers that often invest beyond developing projects, collecting data, analyzing data, and presenting data to fellow researchers, it is imperative to develop strategies that translate research into action. One method to translate research into action is through disaster education programming that uses a bottom-up community approach to present key information needed to move throughout the disaster cycle. Early investing in community capacity building like that of disaster education trainings can help to increase an individual's knowledge, attitudes, preparedness, and skills to undergo the disaster cycle as presented in Semien and Nance (2019).

While much of the disaster education literature agrees that disaster education encourages trainees to take steps to mitigate and prepare for a disaster prior to its onset is one key to hazardous risk reduction, conducting regular workshops are often expensive and time consuming (Karanci et al., 2005). In some cases, access to the training as well as the resources administered at the training is also limited for socially vulnerable groups due to the time and place the training is hosted. Socially vulnerable groups often lack the transportation, money, and the time commitment to attend these sessions (Arroyo and Zigler, 1995). In other cases, the information presented at the trainings may be culturally inappropriate and may not speak to the social disparities faced by various ethnic or religious groups during a disastrous event. In addition, resources provided may be designed and presented in one language and at one educational level, decreasing the likelihood that those in attendance will understand the information presented.

In a technologically advancing world many have argued that in-person trainings can be eliminated and replaced with virtual/online sessions. In fact, organizations like The American Red Cross, Federal Emergency Management Agency (FEMA), and the Department of Homeland Security (DHS) and others have moved much of their

DOI: 10.4324/9781003177005-8

information online. While transitioning from a physical presence to a virtual presence is increasing due to pandemics, convenience, and reduced cost there is still a limitation that prevents vulnerable populations like the poor, elderly, and the computer illiterate from accessing this information (Wingate et al., 2007). Although it is possible for community residents to request physical copies of the material, this also comes with a limitation regarding usability (Sutton and Tierney, 2006). In addition, these materials may not be comprehensive nor relatable enough to ensure that community members have a complete understanding of the execution needed to plan and prepare for a disaster (Paton and Johnston, 2001; Suda, 2000). One of the best ways to ensure both access and usability is to develop community tailored, comprehensive, and hands-on workshops that utilize physical disaster preparedness kits to ensure that participants develop a clear understanding needed to prepare for a disaster (Karanci et al., 2005; Paton and Johnston, 2001).

There are few resources available that guide practitioners, researchers, and community leaders using step-by-step best practices for educating high risk communities. The remaining section of this book seeks to provide step-by-step instruction on how to implement a disaster training workshop that is community tailored and hands-on with limited financial resources. The information will be presented using the case study community of Geismar, Louisiana following the K.A.P.S. Model outlined in Part II of this book. This Part is divided into three chapters: Chapter 6: Building a K.A.P.S. Community Training; Chapter 7: Implementing and Evaluating a K.A.P.S. Community Training, and Chapter 8: Epilogue. The intended goal of Part III is to provide resources and tools for hosting a K.A.P.S. training.

BOX P.2 K.A.P.S. LEGACY SPOTLIGHT 2

Amos Favorite
Environmental Activist

Your father was an integral part of the environmental justice movement in Geismar, Louisiana—what does that legacy mean to you?

Maliaka Favorite: His actions taught me to consider the environment in all my actions. While I cannot make giant changes, I realize that we, as his children, can be conscious of our actions, and we can support environmental issues in our community.

Tamu Favorite: I admired my father growing up. I was encouraged by him because where most people would look at a something and say somebody should do something about that, my dad was a person who did something about those things. I remember when he [successfully advocated] to stop [industrial] trucks [carrying chemicals] from passing in front of the school and front of the neighborhoods. He was a papa bear that stood up for his family, his environment and political issues affecting the community.

Why do you think it was important for him to take up his journey?

Maliaka Favorite: Dad was always a leader in the community, when he saw injustice, he felt it was his duty as a citizen to do what he could to make a positive difference in the area. He realized that the chemical pollution was harmful to the environment as well as to the people living in the area, this realization catapulted him to act to instigate change.

Tamu Favorite: He was a person who said to himself "Well, I gotta do something …". He was more of an action person. He didn't just see a wrong. He did something about it and he didn't hesitate, he would get involved with an issue so he could make a difference.

How did his legacy impact where you are today?

Maliaka Favorite: His legacy helped me to be conscious of environmental issues, and to do what I can to further his legacy of environmental responsibility. The land cannot lobby for change but we as humans can lobby and act on behalf of the land and the environment.

Tamu Favorite: I like to take care of the earth myself—my dad was very much into taking care of the environment. I feel like I was influenced by my father in that area and when it comes to people. While in New York I taught the formerly incarcerated life skills for rehabilitation into society. My dad believed that you can't just complain, but you must make a difference which is where I guess I took after him in that area. Recently, after the horrible incident with George Floyd my church members and I held a lot of classes on multiracial experiences to really help people understand on both ends what it's like to live in a world that is multiracial. I grew up in Louisiana, so I know living here is very different than living in New York City, but it was very important for me that I was willing to talk with people about these issues. My comment was: I'm willing to talk to you if you were willing to search yourself and question yourself. Ask: Where do you fall short when it comes to racial issues? I questioned myself as a woman of color… so it's important that as a white person to question yourself as well ask yourself where do you fall short? I think it's very important that everybody should have questioned themselves to see what they can change.

Do you remember what it was like as a child watching your dad fight for his family? Can you describe that?

Maliaka Favorite: I was always proud of Daddy's leadership in the community. I learned from him to take an active interest in the issues confronting our community. When I saw the changes he helped to instigate I realized that action could make a difference. I remember having to get water from water stations in Gonzales because our water was polluted. I was so proud when Daddy helped to make it possible for Geismar to get clean water from Baton Rouge.

Tamu Favorite: Absolutely, I started school before the schools were integrated in Ascension Parish, Louisiana and I remember back in first grade, my dad was upset because I came home with raggedy books. The thing is the black schools would get the second-hand books. The other kids in the white schools they were getting, you know, brand new books. My dad was very upset about that so he fought to get us new books. Maliaka was the first person from our community to integrate the public system and of that, the KKK burned a cross in our yard, which is... which was very frightening. My father and my oldest brother would sit up at night with shotguns to protect the house and it was crazy. It was frightening but it was just how it was back then.

If you had to give advice to someone who is currently in your family's shoes — what would that advice be?

Maliaka Favorite: Never close your eyes and wait for someone else to resolve problems. Be a leader for change.

    Tamu Favorite: To make a difference, be willing to ask questions and try to do something about the situation. Don't just complain and don't surrender to defeat. Be willing to go to meetings ... a lot of times in this community people refused to go to meetings. My dad was that person who would go to and lead meetings. He would lead meetings. So now Maliaka, my other sister, and I will go to the environmental meetings, to make sure things are going properly and running smoothly within our community.

How did his role in advocacy impact your family and what is some advice you would give to another family in your position?

Maliaka Favorite: My advice to other families would be to keep up with the local and national news. Don't be ignorant of what is happening in your community and in the world. You never know when you will see an opportunity to become an instrument of change. Too often people find out after the fact what is happening to their community, by then it is too late to act against negative situations. I would encourage young and old to watch the news, read the paper, be in the know of what is going on around you. When you see a problem, report it and then be an active participant in making a difference.

    Tamu Favorite: In our community everyone takes a job in the industrial plant because its good money but they're not thinking about their future, their health. Ten years to 20 years they may be suffering from cancer or some other type of health issue. Don't just take a job just because it's good money. Really think about what and where you are working now and where your family is living while you're working there at the plant.

    My dad was also big on education and big on making a difference for yourself. Daddy encouraged us to go to college.

Learn more about Malaika Favorite: https://malaikafavorite.artspan.com/home
Learn more about Tamu Favorite: https://www.tamufavorite.com/

CHAPTER 6

Building a K.A.P.S. Community Training

....

The first K.A.P.S. training was developed and implemented in 2017 as part of a research study that examined the effectiveness of a tailor-based disaster preparedness training program on individuals from a multi-hazard community. The research expanded the hypothesis by Muttarak and Lutz (2014: 1), which states that "societies can develop the most effective long-term defense against the dangers of climate change by strengthening human capacity, primarily through education." The original project operationalized the hypothesis of Muttarak and Lutz (2014) by seeking to increase capacity through trainings designed to increase knowledge, enhance risk perception, improve readiness, increase cognitive and problem-solving skills (Semien and Nance, 2019).

This operationalization was completed by implementing two adaptations to the original Muttarak and Lutz (2014) framework. The first adaptation used a tailor-based approach to develop content for the training program that included specific and relatable material from the community of interest. The second adaptation used a constructivist instructional method that incorporated hands-on and repeated skill building exercises designed to increase participants' ability to perform the tasks implemented in the curriculum. Our constructivist teaching methods are based on an educational model advanced by Paulo Friere. This model is outlined in Box 6.1. Ultimately the goal of the initial study was to listen, educate, and empower individuals from the community to mitigate and prepare for a disaster before its onset using the K.A.P.S. Model (Bassier et al., 2008).

DOI: 10.4324/9781003177005-9

BOX 6.1 K.A.P.S. FEATURED MODEL 7

Paulo Freire's Critical Pedagogy
Author: Paulo Freire, Ph.D.
Freire Institute

Model Definition

Critical pedagogy is a social movement and an approach to teaching that centers the background, experience, knowledge, and situation of the learner with learning goals established collaboratively by learner and teacher. Critical pedagogy asserts that teaching is political, not neutral. Students can be empowered or disempowered by the curriculum; some can even be harmed.

> The teacher is of course an artist but being an artist does not mean that he or she can make the profile, can shape the students. What the educator does in teaching is to make it possible for the students to become themselves.
>
> Paulo Freire, *We Make the Road by Walking: Conversations on Education and Social Change*

Model Summary

Paulo Freire (1921–1997) was an influential educator and philosopher from Brazil. Freire was a leader in the critical pedagogy movement, which focused on educating the poor so they could vote and otherwise fully participate in society. His first work was *Education as the Practice of Freedom* (1967), and his most famous work was *Pedagogy of the Oppressed* (1968). Freire was invited to teach at Harvard in 1969, which corresponded with his 10-year period of exile from Brazil due to the 1964 military takeover of the government.

> One cannot expect positive results from an educational or political action program which fails to respect the particular view of the world held by the people. Such a program constitutes cultural invasion, good intentions notwithstanding.
>
> Paulo Freire, *Pedagogy of the Oppressed*

Why Feature Critical Pedagogy?

Similarly to the K.A.P.S. Model, the Critical Pedagogy Model is grounded in the idea that students should be engaged citizens who can improve their lives and communities. The more an individual is equipped with knowledge and skills to advocate on their own behalf, the more successful they will be in advocating on behalf of their own community issues. The best advocate is the one who has experienced the greatest challenges.

Visit the Freire Institute at https://www.freire.org/ to learn more about Critical Pedagogy and Dr. Freire.

While increasing the capacity of individuals living within the community to effectively respond to disasters is not a new phenomenon, the K.A.P.S. Model uses a novel approach to address the weakness and challenges of the typical community training. Typically, trainings are developed with the technical expert in mind, as compared to the individuals living in the community. While these trainings are often filled with technical knowledge and information needed to proceed through the disaster cycle, they often lack local indigenous knowledge (Olsson and Folke, 2001). Local indigenous knowledge is often inclusive of generational preparedness practices that are orally passed down as climatic changes increase within the region. Conventional trainings often exclude local indigenous knowledge because of the lack of support from professional or scientific research (Mercer et al., 2009; Olsson and Folke, 2001). The exclusion of local indigenous knowledge is a widespread practice in many community trainings, and as a result the information lacks the perspective of the community and often goes unheeded due to the inability of participants to relate to the concepts discussed in the training (Mercer et al. 2009; Yli-Pelkonen and Kohl, 2005).

To make training that is more responsive to multi-hazard socially vulnerable communities, the K.A.P.S. curriculum focuses on disasters that are common to the community, describes disaster impacts, and identifies mitigation/preparedness strategies that can be taken in advance (Wells, 2013). This curriculum also addresses negative perceptions, misconceptions, and stresses as well as highlights key community vulnerabilities, ways to stay informed about disasters, and key community contacts (Wells, 2013). Finally, the curriculum incorporates scenario-based training that re-emphasizes the tools, resources, and techniques that can be used in the event a disaster.

Ultimately the K.A.P.S. curriculum seeks to go beyond previous training that only compiled generic emergency preparedness knowledge. We developed a five-step process to implement the K.A.P.S. training: (1) profile the community, (2) recruit stakeholders, (3) request fiscal support, (4) recruit participants, and (5) implement the training. Each step allowed us to study in-depth the community of interest before developing and implementing training materials. The five steps are presented in detail, with best practices, and practical worksheets included in the remaining sections of this chapter, these resources can be adapted to support training development in other communities.

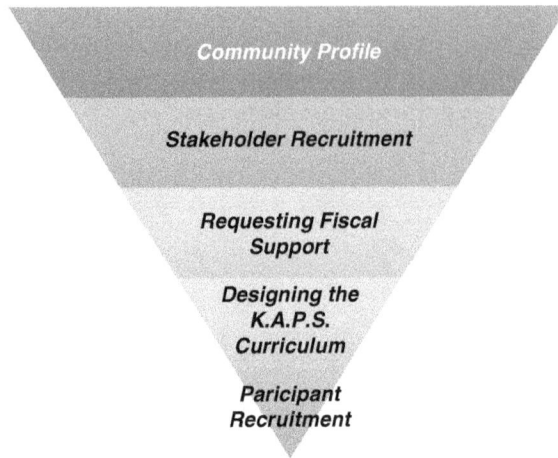

FIGURE 6.1 Bottom-up approach to implementing a K.A.P.S. community training

STEP 1: COMMUNITY PROFILE

The first step to implementing a K.A.P.S. disaster training is to profile the community and develop a written community profile report. Profiling a community provides information about the community's past, present, and future conditions. Ultimately these conditions can lay the groundwork for understanding the social, cultural, political, and economic landscapes that embody the community (EPA, n.d.). This landscape is the foundation for understanding the community's uniqueness as well as its historical challenges and successes (Fernandez and Ahmed, 2019). The purpose of the profile is to identify community-wide trends and vulnerabilities to determine which mitigation metrics may be plausible to present to the community during the implementation of the K.A.P.S. instructional model.

In implementing the K.A.P.S. Model, the process of profiling the community allows the workshop coordinator to learn about the community's multi-hazard risk profile by seeking to understand the community's history and culture, its socio-demographic status, as well as its experience with past disasters (Semien and Nance, 2019). The first step to undergoing this learning experience is to conduct interviews with practitioners, disaster specialists, and local community leaders. The main idea is to engage with people within the community as well as experts from around the country to develop a tailored training approach for the community of interest. Using both local and scientific knowledge allows for the development of a community specific K.A.P.S. curriculum (Mercer et al., 2009). Early profiling can also increase the receptibility of the information while reducing feelings of anger, isolation, and confusion by the community members (Liming, 2021). In general, the more time a presenter devotes to the early analysis of the community, the more likely community participation will increase, regardless of the relationship that the instructor or program manager may or may not have with the community (Bassier et al., 2008).

Typically profiling a community is completed using secondary data collected from online resources, and/or anthropological study (Bassier et al., 2008). The profile often contains sections related to the communities' background, geographic description, population demographics, and political and economic background (EPA, n.d). In implementing the K.A.P.S. Model we expanded the common community profile to contain the following sections: (I.) Executive Summary, (II.) Introduction and Case Study, (III.) Geographic/Topographical Analysis, (IV.) Population Assessment, (V.) Political, Social, and Economic Conditions, (VI.) Housing Conditions, (VII.) Transportation, (VIII.) Community Infrastructure, (IX.) Disaster and the Environment, (X.) Conclusion, and (XI.) References. This adaptation helped us to document the community in its entirety.

Parts of the Community Profile

I. Executive Summary

The first section of the profile is the executive summary. The *Executive Summary* provides a summation of the material in the profile. This section should be written last to ensure that it encompasses the necessary components of the report. The executive summary should be no more than a page and should highlight the important points of each topic area within the community profile. The easiest way to write an executive summary is to summarize the main idea from each section into one sentence.

II. Introduction and Case Study

The second section is the *Introduction* and the *Case Study*. The introduction subsection briefly presents the project that the team seeks to implement as well as introducing the overall purpose of the study. The introduction should include a summary of the reason for completing this analysis as well as an explanation of the intended outcome, and how the information will be used in the future. The introduction should also lead to presenting the background of the community or the *Case Study*.

The *Case Study* sub-section of the profile provides a comprehensive history and background of the community of interest. This section thoroughly identifies the community origin, historical injustices, changes in development, and a summation of present-day activities. It is important to also highlight challenges that the community faces and any methods used by the community to overcome those challenges. A brief discussion of the community values, attitudes, and knowledge should also be included in this session. This analysis can help identify cultural sensitivities and the need for multiple languages. Conducting a thorough assessment of historical challenges and the current climate of the community can help an instructor determine best practices on how to approach the people living within the community.

Resources that can help develop a strong *Case Study* Section include:

1. City website
2. County and Paris websites

3. State websites
4. The local library
5. Archived newspapers
6. Local historians

III. Geographic/Topographical Analysis

The *Geographic/Topographical* section of the profile provides a comprehensive assessment of the community's physical landscape. This section contains information regarding the square mileage, the community's boundary lines, and natural elevations. Also in this section is a description of the communities' natural resources, flood zones, types of terrain, and soil. Maps should be included in this section that visually depict the community and its relation to the region and/or state in which the community is located. This analysis can help to determine what environmental hazards the community is susceptible to experiencing. Identifying the community's susceptibility to specific hazards before training can help the facilitator determine what preparation and mitigation activities should be included in the instructional portion of the training.

Resources to complete the *Geographic/Topographical Analysis* section are:

1. Geographic Information System (GIS)
2. ESRI Community Analyst
3. Census Geographical Data
4. Google Earth
5. Local Hazard Mitigation or Emergency Response Plans

IV. Population Assessment

The *Population Assessment* section of the profile provides a thorough assessment of who lives in the community. The information collected and presented in this section should include a comprehensive list of all sociodemographic statistics like gender, race, ethnicity, age, income, education, marital status, and family size. When presenting this information, it is important to present the information in comparison to the region, county, and/or state to offer a full picture of sociodemographic relationships. Having a full comparative picture can identify pockets of populations that may be socially vulnerable, increasing their susceptibility to a hazardous event. Using a geographic information system to map the sociodemographics can also provide a visual that identifies specific neighborhoods or regions where socially vulnerable groups may be located. This is a critical section of the community profile because understanding who is in the community and where these groups are located can add a layer of tailored support that can build resilience among these groups.

Resources to complete the *Population Assessment* include:

1. Census.data.gov
2. Socialexplorer.com

3. City, County, and Parish websites
4. State websites
5. Geographic Information Systems (GIS)
6. Savi.org
7. Google/Google Scholar
8. The Center for Disease Control Social Vulnerability Indicators website

V. Political, Social and Economic Conditions

The *Political* subsection of the *Political, Social and Economic* section provides information on the political capital that exists within the community. Political capital often refers to power, access, and engagement (Beaulieu, 2014; Brett and Oviatt, 2013; Dash, 2013; Wallace and Wolf, 2006). In the event of a disaster, those that are more politically connected may be first to receive disaster-related information or are more likely to be the first to have their essential utilities restored (Bullard and Wright, 2009; Enarson and Fordham, 2000; Bullard, Johnson, and Torres, 2009). This section also provides information regarding the government and administrative jurisdictions, political regions, and sectors. In this subsection it is also important to identify possible political stakeholders who may help to support or advocate for the instructional course among residents as they may be able to help recruit community members.

The *Social* subsection of the *Political, Social, and Economic* section provides information on the social capital that may exist in the community. Social capital is often referred to as the "glue" that causes individuals to become bonded, bridged, or linked to each other (Beaulieu, 2014; Nakagawa and Shaw, 2004; Brett and Oviatt, 2013). These networks bring individuals together creating larger groups that build trust and provide greater access to resources (Bolin and Bolton, 1986; Chamlee-Wright and Storr, 2011). Increased resilience occurs when individuals become involved in groups and/or networks with connections to resources and other assets that the individuals alone may otherwise lack (Xiao et al., 2018, Kim and Zakour, 2017). This section includes a list of nonprofit organizations, social networks, and churches responsible for the social well-being of the community. It is important to note that these groups are often good stakeholders.

The *Economic* subsection of the *Political, Social, and Economic* section provides information on the overall economy of the community as well as the types of businesses contributing to the economy. This information is imperative to understand because the disaster literature states that businesses often serve as economic powerhouses for many socially vulnerable communities (Tierney, 1997; Xiao et al., 2018). Businesses often provide a layer of economic resources needed to fund investment programs, projects, ideas, and construction projects (Beaulieu, 2014; Scandlyn et al., 2013; Brett and Oviatt, 2013). These organizations can also serve as great allies and stakeholders for supporting instructional programs. This section includes a list of businesses and business networks responsible for the economic well-being of the community.

Resources to complete *Political, Social and Economic* are:

1. State, County, and City political boundaries
2. Policymap.com
3. Yellow Pages
4. Census.gov
5. USA.com
6. Local Chamber of Commerce

VI. Housing Conditions

The *Housing* section of the community profile provides information on the housing stock of the community. This section often includes information on the ownership status, average age of the home, the purchase cost of the home as well as whether the properties are rental or owner-occupied. This information is important to include in the profile because it can provide an early assessment of properties that may be at risk during a hazard event.

Resources to complete the *Housing Section* are:

1. Census.data.gov
2. The County and State assessor's office
3. HUD.gov

VII. Transportation

The *Transportation* section of the community profile presents information about the types of road networks that are in the community. In this section, main thruway routes are identified, as well as who is responsible for their maintenance. Here evacuation routes are also identified stating which routes should and should not be taken during a disaster. This section may also present information on the availability of public transportation as well as the ability to access transportation given an emergency. Secondary data can also be used to determine the types of vehicles common in this area and how many households have access to those vehicles. This information is important to include in the profile because it can provide an assessment of how many individuals may/may not have access to transportation in the event of a disaster.

Resources to complete the *Transportation* section include:

1. Department of Motor Vehicles
2. Census.data.gov
3. County and State office of transportation
4. County and State office of homeland security

VIII. Community Infrastructure

The *Community Infrastructure* section of the community profile presents information regarding critical infrastructure like sewerage, water, and electricity sources.

This section also includes information about mass shutoff protocols in the event of a hazardous event as well as outlining the responsibility of individuals living within the community. A list of utility providers with their contact information should be included in this section. It is important to identify which providers' information should be included in the training material to distribute the individuals to be used in the case of emergency. Including this information will help to identify point of contacts and services provided given an emergency.

Resources to complete *Community Infrastructure* section include:

1. County and City public works office
2. County and City engineering office (if separate)
3. Utility (i.e. sewage, water, electric, gas) providers servicing the target area
4. County and City floodplain management office

IX. Disaster and the Environment

The next section is *Disaster and the Environment*, which presents critical information regarding the types of hazards the community is at risk for being impacted. In this section, we recommend identifying past hazard events such as flooding, hurricanes, tornadoes, and chemical spills. Including this information provides a unique opportunity that presents community specific hazard related information that can thoroughly help to prepare the community. Environmental risk analysis should also be conducted and presented in this section.

This analysis should examine the human effects on the air, soil, and water while critically determining the community risk given a hazard event. A health impact analysis can help to determine common health inequities in the region and the distribution of those affected within the population. This analysis can also help to identify pollutants, health disparities leading to nutritional access, as well as occupational safety and health disparities. This information is important to include because it identifies the population that may need additional attention within the community that may be at risk during a hazard event.

Resources to complete the *Disaster and the Environment* section are:

1. National Hurricane Center
2. National Oceanic Atmospheric Association
3. Federal Emergency Management Agency
4. floodfactor.com
5. Internet search engines for disasters impacting the community of interest
6. Environmental Protection Agency Toxic Release Inventory (TRI)
7. TRI Pollution Prevention tool
8. TRI Explorer
9. Environfacts
10. Risk Screening Environmental Indicators (RSEI)
11. My Right to Know Application (myRTK)

12. National Institute of Health
13. County Health Ranking system
14. The Center for Disease Control Community Health Assessment

X. Conclusion

The final section of the community profile is a brief conclusion that summarizes the major components of the information presented in the report as well as a list of references that was used to create the report.

Validating the Community Profile

While we recognize community profiling can require a large time commitment, to complete each step is imperative to understand the major landscapes that exist within the community prior to conducting a K.A.P.S. training. Much of the data for the community profile can be collected from secondary data sources. It is important to validate the collected information through informal/formal interviews and/or community wide surveys. It is also important to use this phase of the model to establish early connections with key community stakeholders. These early established connections can help to validate the secondary information collected for the profile to ensure that all the community challenges have been identified and presented correctly. Validation is a major part in implementing the model to ensure that collected information is accurate prior to executing the model.

STEP 2: STAKEHOLDER RECRUITMENT

After profiling a community, it is important to build partnerships with individuals and/or groups who can become a key stakeholder in implementing a K.A.P.S. workshop. Stakeholders are individuals or "groups who have expert knowledge that should be considered, [and who are] essential to the implementation of resulting policies, [programs,] and/or have an interest in the outcome of the work" (Burton et al., 2008: 12). Building early partnerships with stakeholders allows for a system of checks and balances which can supply a collaborative opportunity to verify, share, and distribute information to those living/working in the community (Gibson and Hayunga, 2006).

In disaster research, historical methods to acquire stakeholder support have been centered around technical expertise which often ignores local traditional knowledge and existing socio/political power dynamics (Chandrasekhar, 2012). This is problematic because both the collected information as well as selected stakeholders will lack a clear understanding of the communities' strengths, weaknesses, and adaptive behavior. Choosing a broad range of stakeholders can help to eliminate gaps in understanding community behaviors as well as reduce the lack of trust common between those new to the community and those indigenous to the community.

While it is imperative to develop a large list of key stakeholders early on, it is important to find individuals and/or groups who operate on both a local and a national level from the very beginning (Bassier et al., 2008: 12). It is also important to choose individuals and/or groups who have previously worked within the community as well as those who have no experience with the community but can offer a broad range of technical knowledge. Choosing a broad range of stakeholders can ensure the validity of the information collected as well as help recruit participants to actively take part in the workshop.

Types of Stakeholders

In implementing the original K.A.P.S. case study we ultimately chose stakeholders from five groups: (1) technical experts, (2) practitioners, (3) local community politicians, (4) business owners, (5) nonprofit organizations and community-based organizations. We selected these groups because they could offer validation of secondary data collected and recruitment support needed to implement the workshop.

- *Technical experts* are those individuals and/or groups who are specialists in a given field and can offer a specific knowledge or expertise (Williams, 2001). In the case of K.A.P.S. we sought technical experts who had experience in the field of environmental justice, hazard/disaster research, and community-based research.
- *Practitioners* are those individuals whose profession encompasses the ability to turn knowledge and/or theory into actionable programs to increase the capacity of community members (Williams, 2001; Abarquez and Murshed, 2004). In the case of K.A.P.S. we sought practitioners whose professions were in the field of emergency management and public safety.
- *Local politicians* are individuals who are actively involved in the administrative, legislative, judicial, and other public affairs of the community (Hanssen, 2010). In the case of K.A.P.S. we sought senators and representatives who had a historical or current invested interest in the overall environmental health of the community. We particularly sought those who had advocated for resources and policy changes to ensure the health of those living within the multi-hazard community of Geismar, Louisiana.
- *Business owners* are those who own for-profit entities that have an economic interest in the success of the community (Runyan, 2006). In the case of K.A.P.S. we particularly sought those who could offer fiscal support as well as those who could supply information regarding the communities' adaptive behaviors to repeated onset of disasters.
- *Nonprofit organizations leaders* are those that operate not-for-profit entities like churches, social groups, and community organizations, whose mission it is to support the socioeconomic advancement within vulnerable communities (Chikoto et al., 2013). Leaders of nonprofit organizations are pivotal to obtain because they often serve as gatekeepers to residents, businesses, and organizations existing within the larger community (Chikoto-Schultz et al., 2018). These

individuals and/or groups can also play a key role in ensuring that community members are aware of trainings as well as encourage their attendance.

Methods to Obtaining Stakeholder Support

There are many methods to identify and solicit stakeholder support. In implementing the K.A.P.S. study we choose to primarily write letters and e-mails to potential stakeholders. The letter introduced the project and asked for their support in completing the study. See below for the example letter used in the original study. We also used phone canvasing, social media, and in person visits to entities who could not be reached by e-mail using an adapted version of the e-mail script.

BOX 6.2 K.A.P.S FEATURED PRACTITIONER SPOTLIGHT 4

Monique Harden, Esq.
Deep South Center for Environmental Justice (DSCEJ)

What is your area of Specialty?

I am a lawyer and an advocate who has over 30 years of experience fighting with and on behalf of frontline communities.

How did you get into this work?

I originally entered this work because I saw firsthand how communities had so much staked against them. They deserve to live well and free.

How have you worked to address the problem of marginalized communities in your career?

My role in the community is often to help community members understand power and how to advocate for themselves. In the past I have collaborated with communities to develop their capacity to build strategies to address environmental issues.

What would you wish you could have done differently now that you looked back at the landscape of the field?

There's always that one case that you wish you could have managed differently. In handling that case I wish I would have done more work and had a better outcome for the small frontline community. Today this community is ravaged by chemical plants and much of its history and its descendants are lost.

What is the biggest advice you have for other practitioners?

- Connect with other advocates
- Respect and care for other people
- Be accountable and communicate properly

How should people become more involved in these issues?

If you want to be part of social change, learn about the community. Meet people at the community level. Be proactive and be an overall learner. Leverage what people already do and who is currently in the community. Don't be afraid to connect with different people and build your own professional network.

"This work is challenging—have fun when you can."

Learn more about Monique Harden at https://www.dscej.org/our-story/our-team/monique-harden-esq

Assessing Stakeholders

After selecting stakeholders, the next step is to schedule an informal meeting with each individual or group. The goal of this meeting is to get to know the stakeholder by presenting the goals of the project. After the goals of the project have been identified it is important to also use the guiding questions on the next page to perform an initial assessment to ensure that the potential individual/group is a good fit for the implementation of the project.

Formal and informal interviews should be administered to obtain information needed to profile the community, such as information on cultural background, community history, as well as past impacts of natural and anthropogenic disasters (as described in Step 1). Interviews should also be conducted to obtain information on strategies to implement the workshop. The interviews should be administered to disaster professionals, first responders, community members, and disaster preparedness organizations by phone, zoom, and/or in person. Introductory e-mails should also be used to invite stakeholders to take part in the workshop and/or learn more about the workshop. Ideally interviews should last approximately 15 to 30 minutes. Before performing the interview, it is a good idea to pre-test every question to reduce the opportunity for errors and ambiguous and unanswerable questions (Babbie, 2013: 251). This assessment can be completed informally using a conversational tone as compared to a formal interview style. This is also a good time to have the stakeholder verify information that was collected and placed in the community profile in Step 1. If the study is being conducted for university research purposes, the study methods and procedures will need to be submitted to a university institutional review board (IRB) to receive approval to work with human subjects.

Stakeholder support can vary from being a full partner in completing the project to just offering time to verify secondary data. It is important to never underestimate stakeholder support regardless of how little or extensive the support may seem. In implementing the initial K.A.P.S. trainings we received stakeholder support from all five stakeholder categories listed above. Each individual and group offered different information and resources which was collectively implemented and placed and used to formulate the entire study. The below table provides a brief outline of the stakeholders and a brief description of their purpose.

Stakeholders		
Local	The local library	A place to hold community workshops.
Local	The parish office of Homeland Security and Emergency Preparedness	The parish office can provide key political connections, informational brochures, and other sources of information.
Local	Parish Sheriff's Office	Build a network for establishing community resources.
Local	Local Fire Department	A place to hold community workshops and build a network for establishing community resources.
Local	Local Churches and Faith-Based Institutions	A place to hold community workshops and build a network of community members.
Local	Nonprofits (i.e. American Red Cross, The United Way)	Request informational packets, brochures, and health kits to help the community build awareness regarding disaster preparedness.
National	Federal Emergency Management Agency	Request informational packets, brochures, and books to help the community build awareness in regard to disaster preparedness.
National	National Center for Disaster Preparedness	Request informational packets, brochures, and books to help the community build awareness regarding disaster preparedness.

FIGURE 6.2 Example list of key community stakeholders

STEP 3: REQUESTING FISCAL SUPPORT

Access to the financial capital required to design and implement training programs is typically limited, especially in multi-hazard communities. Financial capital consists of the economic resources needed to fund programs, projects, and ideas (Beaulieu, 2014; Scandlyn et al., 2013; Brett and Oviatt, 2013). As a result, few public organizations regularly host programs designed to train members of the community to prepare for a disaster.

In many cases the design and implementation of training programs like K.A.P.S. are left in the hands of nonprofit organizations to host, who may also have limited financial capital to support the training program. Small nonprofit organizations who are led by and/or support small minority communities often experience a disproportionate ability to access additional funding sources. This may be the result of a lack of access to funding nonprofit/donation sources, the inability to meet various eligibility requirements, or lack of knowledge and skills needed to successfully complete the application. These inabilities make it extremely hard for small minority-led nonprofit to receive funding to support both the organizational and community preparedness. While there is a great need to expand sources for funding and donations, the K.A.P.S. program instituted a novel approach to acquire funding to support the design and implementation of the training program (Pipa, 2006; Chikoto-Schultz et al., 2018).

In designing and implementing the K.A.P.S. training program we decided to request fiscal and physical support from the list of stakeholders, described in Step 2. We first begin by making a list of all items needed to ensure the success of the workshop with the dollar amount needed to purchase the item (see Figure 6.3). We than separated the items in the list into three categories (1) items that could be purchased in store, (2) hot food, and (3) physical material needed to host the workshop.

Category	Needed Supplies	Location	Estimated Price (2018)	Donated (Y/N)
1	Extension cord	Walmart	$5.00	
1	30 disaster kits	Walmart	$1,000.00	Y
1	30 disaster binders	Office Depot	$500.00	Y
1	30 pens	Walmart	$5.00	Y
1	Activity boxes	Walmart	$100.00	Y
2	Donuts/milk	Southern Maid Donut Shelley's Donuts	$20.00	Y
3	Conference room	Geismar Library	Free	Y
3	Projector with cords	Office Depot	$2,000.00	Y
3	Laptop	K.A.P.S. Team	$1,000.00	Y
3	PowerPoint slides	K.A.P.S. Team	Free	N/A
3	Camera	Office Depot	$100.00	Y
3	Tripod	Office Depot	$40.00	Y
3	Informational brochures	FEMA Warehouse https://www.ready.gov/publications	Free	Y

FIGURE 6.3 Supplies required to host K.A.P.S. workshop

Once the items were properly categorized, we used the letter in Appendix B3 to both obtain fiscal sponsors as well as request that they purchase and/or donate the items needed to make the workshop a success. All items that could be purchased in-store were placed on a Wal-Mart wish list for ease of purchasing by fiscal sponsors. We included the Walmart Wish List link in the letter to solicit support. Using this method, all of the required supplies and materials were donated, including a location for hosting the workshop. While acquiring funding to host trainings and workshops alone may be challenging, soliciting the support of the larger community in which the event will be held offers a level of mutual benefit. In this manner community businesses, nonprofit organizations, and individuals receive free advertisement while the training workshop receives free and/or discounted supplies. This method also creates an opportunity to develop strong community relationships that may be beneficial in the future.

STEP 4: DESIGNING THE K.A.P.S. CURRICULUM

While every practitioner has their own method for designing curriculums, the K.A.P.S. community training primarily uses concept mapping to build the content for the lesson plans. Concept mapping is a qualitative method to consolidate large bodies of information into key focus areas, themes, and subthemes (Babbie, 2013: 396–403). To build the K.A.P.S. lesson plans we looked for themes and subthemes that fit within the four focus areas of K.A.P.S.: Knowledge, Attitudes, Preparedness, and Skills. To identify themes and subthemes we extracted information obtained from literature reviews, the community profile, and community stakeholder interview. To increase reliability and validity we conducted literature reviews comprised of peer reviewed articles, technical reports, as well as best practice reports specific to the field of disaster research.

Themes in the knowledge focus area were centered around building communities to be more resilient pre- and post-disaster impact. In the original study we extracted knowledge-based themes from studies like Karanci and Akşit (2000), in Ankara, Turkey, whose work identified key concepts that are important in teaching disaster preparedness.

Themes in the attitude focus area should be centered around examining community vulnerability. In the original study we extracted attitude-based themes from the community profile, the Ascension Parish Homeland Security Office, and community stakeholder interviews. We also contacted *The Wally Wise Guy* Program, based out of Deer Park Texas, who had previously played a role in educating the youth in the community in years past on preparation for industrial spills.

Themes in the preparedness focus area were centered around determining key community resources to strengthen the community's ability to become resilient. In the original study we extracted preparedness-based themes from FEMA, The American Red Cross, Get Ready NYC, Columbia University's National Center for Disaster Preparedness, and Baton Rouge Citizen Emergency Response Team.

Themes in the skills focus area were centered around roles and strategies that equip individuals to respond to a hazard prior to a disaster. In the original, study skills-based themes were extracted from the "Designing Participatory Workshops" manual produced by the United Nations High Commissioner for Refugees which focused on the "Cognitive, Affective, and Psychomotor" abilities of workshop participants (UNHCR, 2008: 9). The manual provided best practices on developing simulation, brainstorming, case studies, and skills practice exercise game methods to ensure that participants were continuously engaged in the lecture associated with the workshop.

After extracting the four focus areas, themes, and subthemes, we compiled the information into a workable lesson plan. See Figure 6.4 for the concept map used to extract the four focus areas. The lesson plan discussed the importance of having and maintaining a kit, how to stay calm, the importance of having emergency contacts, what to do in the event of a natural disaster, the importance of keeping cash on hand, prescription medication in a generalized area, as well as the resources needed to help with disabilities. Other key areas discussed were evacuation routes, important emergency phone numbers, the various types of emergency alarms, the importance of

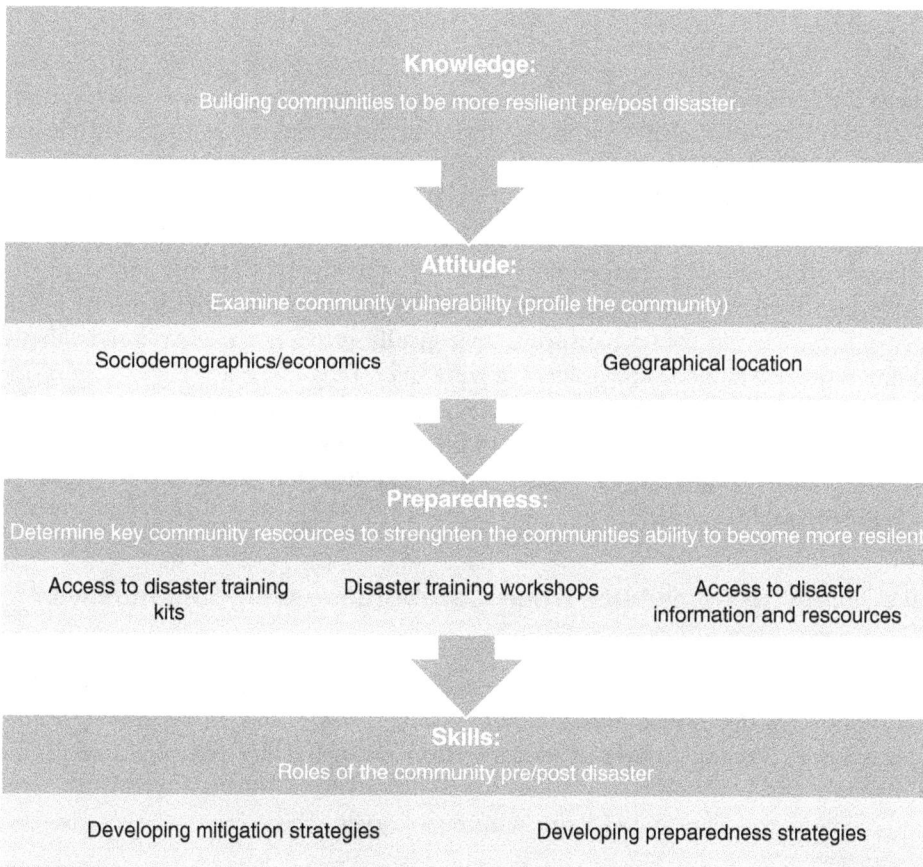

FIGURE 6.4 K.A.P.S. concept map

listening and watching local media for emergency reports, and the importance of time management in the case of an approaching disaster.

STEP 5: PARTICIPANT RECRUITMENT

Participant recruitment is often one of the most difficult steps to building and implementing the K.A.P.S. training program. In the original K.A.P.S. study we initially invited residents of the Geismar, Louisiana who were over the age of 18 to participate using mail solicitation. We acquired addresses for residents from *InfoUSA*. Residents were mailed an invitation to the workshop with a link to RSVP beforehand to confirm attendance. The original invitation read:

> We invite you to participate in a disaster preparedness workshop with before and after questionnaires. You were selected as a participant because you are a current resident of Geismar, Louisiana. Through your consent to participate, you will be trained on the topic of what to do in the case of a natural or manmade disaster.

However, after sending the invitations to community members, we initially only received one response. We then adjusted our recruitment methods to solicit participation to a broader audience by placing flyers within receptive businesses in Geismar, Louisiana including but not limited to supermarkets, cafés, salons, restaurants, churches, and schools (King et al., 2010: 2–3). We also posted flyers to social media outlets Facebook, Twitter, Instagram, Pinterest, and Snapchat. We chose to use social media as a form of advertisement based on a study by Lovejoy and Saxton (2012: 337) who stated the rise of social media has "engendered new paradigms of public engagement." Social media platforms strategically provide a place for individuals, community leaders, and stakeholders to have microblog-like conversations releasing pertinent as well as stimulating information in short blurbs (Lovejoy and Saxton, 2012; Suda, 2000; Banks, 2013). In addition, workshop participants were given upcoming dates to future workshops and asked to distribute the details to interested individuals and/or families.

Five Things to Remember When Collaborating with Communities

1. As an outside practitioner remember "you are a guest in someone else's home." Enter the community with a respect, patience, honesty, and integrity.
2. Understand that every person and/or group plays a role in preventing future casualties. No one group can act completely independently and expect successful interactions.
3. Be willing to listen to and work with people even when technical expertise says otherwise.
4. Be willing to listen first, empower second, engage third, and then drive change.
5. Never dismiss a person's lived experiences … every story matters.

BOX 6.3 K.A.P.S. FEATURED COMMUNITY ACTIVIST 3

Bridgette Murray, R.N.
Founder and Executive Director, Achieving Community Tasks Successfully (ACTS)

What are your primary focus areas in your community?

Through the ACTs organization we focus our mission on providing resources, training and education. We primarily focus on addressing social and environmental justice issues within the Pleasantville Community. Many of our projects involve reducing food insecurity as well as flooding and measuring air quality within our community.

How did you get into this work and how long have you been in this work?

Well, my background is nursing, but I originally became involved in community work because I was working with the Pleasantville Civic League. My involvement led to me eventually becoming president where I worked diligently to engage the community. Around this time, I pursued a master's degree and shortly after I developed the ACTS organization. I have been a community leader in some form for over 35 years.

Do you think that your role as a nurse prepared you for what you're doing now as a community leader?

Yes, I worked in grant writing for a little while and even as a nursing supervisor which equipped me to run this organization. The truth is every experience was trial and error, but it was all good experiences. Throughout every experience I have been able to meet a lot of good people and have gained enough to understand that it's all about service.

How have you built trust within your community?

Trust is a big issue in marginalized communities. For my community it has been important that if I say I am going to be somewhere that I am there. It's important to be accountable and consistent.

Looking back, what do you wish you could have done differently?

The biggest thing I wish I could have done differently is making a bigger generational impact focusing in on certain groups like young people. While many of the senior citizens will come to the meeting there's no guarantee that they are going to do something, but if you get a young person involved, they are more likely to passionately advocate.

How should others face these challenges?

Its important to find good people and organizations to collaborate with because you can't do it by yourself, especially if you have caregiving responsibilities.

How do you balance life and take care of yourself with the amount of work you take on?

- Using discernment to know when to say NO
- Being flexible
- Creating space in my calendar to not work

"I firmly believe that every experience I engaged in helped to prepare me for the work I am doing today as a community leader."

Learn more about Bridgette Murray and ACTS at: https://www.acts-organization.org/

CHAPTER 7

Implementing and Evaluating a K.A.P.S. Community Training

....

The uniqueness of the K.A.P.S. workshop is that it combines two instructional de-livery methods: traditional lecture and constructivist that encourages participants to retain, recall, and apply information (UNHCR, 2008: 41). The decision to combine instructional delivery methods was based on the desire to facilitate an inclusive learning environment tailored to the three types of learners: visual, auditory, and kinesthetic. This approach challenges participants to increase their knowledge, change their attitude, increase their preparedness, and build their critical thinking skills. The content presented in this chapter explains the process of implementing and evaluating a K.A.P.S. workshop.

SCHEDULING THE WORKSHOP

To increase the likelihood of attendance and community participation, the workshop should be strategically scheduled to avoid conflicts with big community events. In choosing a location, be sure to reach out to community stakeholders to help identify a location that is central and neutral (Bassier et al., 2008). Ensuring that the location is both central and neutral can help to attract a broad range of participants from across the entire community. To encourage equitable opportunities for attendance it is essential to host the workshops at various times throughout the month. This will help to ensure that socially vulnerable individuals have an opportunity to attend the workshop at a convenient time.

THE SIZE OF THE WORKSHOP

The ideal size of the workshop should be between 6 to 30 participants; however, the workshop can be adjusted to fit a larger crowd if additional workshop co-facilitators

DOI: 10.4324/9781003177005-10

FIGURE 7.1 Depiction of how to set up the presentation room

are available. However, if the workshop's intended use is solely for educational purposes the number of participants is not relevant. We also suggest that the workshop seats should be in the shape of a rectangle where the head of the rectangle is the instructor. This allows the instructor to see and engage with all participants equally (See Figure 7.1).

OBTAINING CONSENT

As participants enter the workshop, they should be asked to sign a photo/video release and a *Consent to Participate* form. The photo/video release is a document that permits the workshop facilitator and their team to take photos/videos of participants in the workshop. This form also allows the team to use those photos to support the advertisement or recruitment for additional events. The *Consent to Participate* form is a document that outlines the details of the workshop, making it clear that participation is voluntary, and the participants are free to leave at any time. The consent form should also contain text regarding indemnification. The text should read "participants agree to indemnify or hold harmless the workshop coordinator and the team in the event of an accident and/or negligence that leads to participant injury."

While coordinating a K.A.P.S. workshop is centered around ensuring communities have access to key areas of preparedness, it is also important to protect the K.A.P.S. workshop coordinator and the entire K.A.P.S. team. Each form should be thoroughly explained, the form should be completed and signed by each participant. Participants should not be permitted to participate in the workshop until all consent forms have been completed and turned in. In addition, participants should also be given an additional form that outlines where participants could receive assistance if discomfort arose while or after participating in the workshop. The practitioner should clearly iterate that participation is optional and that any participant could choose to opt out of the workshop at any time (Babbie, 2013: 32–33), withdrawing any responses, and signed forms.

RISKS AND BENEFITS

Prior to beginning the workshop, the coordinator should articulate the risks and benefits of participation to workshop participants (Babbie, 2013). Articulating these risks and benefits increases transparency between the workshop participants and the workshop coordinator and team. The primary benefit of participation is that the workshop provides each participant with a set of skills and tools needed to increase their ability to respond appropriately in the event of a natural or anthropogenic disaster. This advanced knowledge and skills can lessen the chances of extreme causalities (Paton and Johnson, 2001). The adverse consequences of participation for individuals who have previous experience with disasters are higher than for those who do not. This is because the images and discussions presented in the workshop can trigger psychological reminders of those events. Other risks are the sense of pre-existing dread that can emerge among participants as they learn the depth and breadth of their disaster risks, or the alienation of learning their risk is disproportional based on race, class or other discriminatory reasons which all cause harm.

In articulating these risks, it is important for the workshop coordinator or a member of the team to identify the local emotional and behavioral support available. In the case study of Geismar, Louisiana the K.A.P.S. team provided each participant with a document that identified and provided contact information for the office of *Ascension Parish Counseling Agency* who at the time offered behavioral and emotional support at a low cost of $5.00.

WORKSHOP FLOW

The typical workshop should last approximately 2 hours, with two 10-minute breaks. In the first 15 minutes of the workshop, participants should be asked to complete a pre-survey to determine their knowledge of hurricane kits, natural and human-made disasters relative to the community of interest, as well as their knowledge of what to do/not to do during a disaster (Karanci et al., 2005). In addition, the pre-survey should contain three subsections: preparedness, experience, and sociodemographics/socioeconomics. The preparedness subsection assesses the self-perception of participants' willingness to prepare for disastrous events.

The first 15 minutes should be followed by a 1-hour hands-on lesson on disasters and disaster preparedness. During the workshops, participants should be thoroughly trained by the coordinator on the topic of disaster preparedness using the community tailored K.A.P.S. lesson plans.

The K.A.P.S. lesson plans are grounded in differential and constructive learning techniques which have been shown to increase participant relatability. Differential learning techniques are those that include the incorporation of learning checkpoints and participatory skill-building exercises designed to ensure retention. Following the K.A.P.S. framework the workshop should be divided into four sections (Knowledge, Awareness, Preparedness, and Skill) with each section having a small interactive review section to keep participants focused and engaged.

The four sections of information can be presented using PowerPoint slides or other methods for presenting documentation that contain visuals of disaster-related images, graphs, and tables (UNHCR, 2008). In addition, participants should be given their own personal handbooks with fillable summary sheets that they can complete during the presentation. Providing a workbook increases receptibility and attentiveness, as well as providing participants with resources that can be brought home and continuously assessed.

The skill section is presented at the end of the workshop. This section allows the participants to practice what they learned in the workshop using pre-made scenario sheets and disaster preparedness kits. Examples of these scenarios can be found in the Appendix of this book; these scenarios should be used as a guide to develop community tailored scenarios. In this section participants should be asked to use the items in the kit to solve the scenarios in their personalized workbook. Every group should be given 15 minutes to complete two scenarios. This method allows the co-ordinator to adequately engage each participant using hands-on instructional methods (UNHCR, 2008).

In the final 15 minutes of the workshop, participants should be asked to complete a post workshop survey (Babbie, 2013). The survey should assess four subsections: preparedness, experience, workshop effectiveness, and sociodemographic/socio-economics. To help "the respondents make sense of the [survey]" each section should contain an introductory phase that "introduces each [section] with a short statement concerning its content and purpose" in the same structural manner of the pre-survey (Babbie, 2013: 241).

Take-home Material

Upon completing the workshop, every participant should be given a disaster preparedness kit to take home. Distributing the disaster preparedness kits are an added benefit to hosting the workshop using the K.A.P.S. framework. As an important component of the framework, we believe that if participants are giving their time as well as energy and attention to attend the workshop, it is important as part of the K.A.P.S. Model to reciprocate that effort with a tangible gift that can be used to further increase their knowledge of preparedness.

While in many cases supplying participants with disaster kits and workbooks can be expensive, in the initial K.A.P.S. workshop we solicited support from stake-holders, as described in Chapter 6 in the subsections of Step 2 and 3. We acquired materials to design and construct these kits through a series of donations from local and national stakeholders such as grassroots organizations, local law enforcement offices, the American Red Cross, and local businesses.

FIGURE 7.2 A participant holding a take-home disaster kit and handbook

Items included in each disaster kit included the following:

- Backpack
- Family disaster plan
- Pens/markers
- Flashlight
- Radio
- Matches
- Manual can opener
- Energy foods/crackers
- Plastics utensils
- Bottle of water
- First aid kit (band-aids, antibacterial ointments)
- Toiletries (toothbrush, shampoo, soap, deodorant)
- Hand sanitizer
- Toilet paper
- Towels
- Sunscreen
- Bug spray
- Garbage bags
- Zip-lock bags
- Small tool kit (pocket knife, small screwdriver, scissors)
- Whistle
- Duct tape
- Lysol wipes to go
- Small notebook

- Raincoat
- Particle respirator
- Gloves

Evaluating a K.A.P.S. Inspired Community Training

Conducting a thorough evaluation is the next step following the implementation of the K.A.P.S. community training. Evaluation is the practice of critically assessing a program to improve, increase knowledge, and illustrate value (Patton, 1987; Kirkpatrick and Kirkpatrick, 2016). The remaining sections of this chapter will present: approaches to evaluating K.A.P.S.; understanding the data; preparing the data; analyzing the data; and checking for reliability, validity, and bias.

APPROACHES TO EVALUATING K.A.P.S.

The first step in evaluating a K.A.P.S. training approach is to identify the actionable and measurable learning objectives presented in the training program. Identifying actionable and measurable learning objectives enables the coordinator to effectively communicate the lesson and enables the evaluator to determine if those objectives were met. In implementing the K.A.P.S. workshop there are five main objectives: for the participants: (1) differentiate between human-made and natural disasters, (2) plan and prepare for an human-made and natural disaster, (3) collect and employ supplies in the event of an human-made and natural disaster, (4) identify and access resources needed to respond in the event of a disaster and (5) self-determine usefulness of the training. To evaluate the effectiveness of the K.A.P.S. training to meet these objectives across all of the participants, the program combines both a formative and summative approach to measure the training objectives (Kirkpatrick and Kirkpatrick, 2016).

Types of Evaluation

Formative evaluation focuses on developing and improving the program by identifying weaknesses of the instructional material, methods, or learning objectives (Wang and Wilcox, 2006; Brown and Gerhardt, 2002). This method of evaluation usually occurs throughout the entirety of the training, collecting feedback from the trainee to be used to improve the trainee's knowledge and skills throughout the entirety of the workshop. In implementing the K.A.P.S. workshop, we used strategies like *call and response* to ensure participants were engaged, held discussions to ensure participants were retaining information, performed brief checks to ensure participants were physically and emotionally comfortable, and conducted a skills section that required participants to work in groups and solve simulation exercises. In addition, the workshop coordinator enlisted the support of team members to observe the dynamics of the room. If team members noticed the need for alterations to increase comfortability, those changes were made inconspicuously.

Summative evaluation focuses on training outcomes through measurement and assessment (Wang and Wilcox, 2006; Alvarez et al., 2004). This method of evaluation usually occurs after the training to measure participants' changes in knowledge and skills. In implementing the K.A.P.S. workshop, the workshop coordinator implemented assessment measures using the pre- and post-surveys that addressed all five objectives. In addition, the coordinator incorporated teach-back exercises to ensure participants were able to recall and apply newly acquired knowledge as a result of participating in the workshop (see Figure 7.3 for a visual depiction).

Objectives	Levels of Evaluation		Formative Evaluation Measures			Summative Evaluation Measures		
	Level 1	Level 2	Sub-section Exercises	Call and Response	Skills Exercises (Simulation)	Pre-Survey	Post-Survey	Skills Exercises (Teach-back)
Differentiate between human-made and natural disasters		X	X	X		X	X	
Plan and prepare for an human-made and natural disaster		X	X		X	X	X	X
Collect and employ supplies in the event of human-made and natural disasters		X	X		X	X	X	X
Identify and access resources needed to respond in the event of a disaster		X	X	X	X	X	X	X
Self-determine usefulness of the training	X						X	

FIGURE 7.3 Evaluation measures used in the K.A.P.S. Model

BOX 7.1 K.A.P.S. FEATURED PRACTITIONER SPOTLIGHT 5

Bakeyah Nelson, Ph.D.
Global Initiative Director, Climate Imperative Founder, Community Health Collaborative Consulting

What is your area of specialty?

My area of specialty is primarily evaluation. My role as an evaluator is to assess community-based organizations and offer strategies to increase their capacity.

How did you get into this work?

I grew up in DC, I am not originally from a community that has those [environmental] issues. I remember the first time I saw people and children playing next to facilities that are harmful to people's health. It was a turning factor that changed the trajectory of my career.

What types of resources and tools do you use to increase the capacity of marginalized communities?

- Community meetings
- Evaluation planning
- Provide trainings to encourage leadership, communication, and advocacy skills

What would you wish you could have done differently now that you looked back at the landscape of the field?

Early on in my career I collaborated with a small community in Houston, Texas and I wasn't able to produce a few deliverables that would have been beneficial for the community. From this experience I have learned to get comfortable with failure.

What is the biggest advice you have for other practitioners?

Even with great passion and evaluation you may still not see the results of your work or the work of your partners. It is important to accept that this work is an ongoing struggle and there will always be a heaviness to it – just do the best you can.

What are some activities you use to "self-care?"

- Exercise: being out in nature, recreational activities.
- Alone time/quality time: think about what you could have done differently.
- Talking to peers to decompress: friends/colleagues that understand the work.
- Listen to audiobooks – about different topics on leadership, mental health, how to manage your emotions and mood.

  "Don't take yourself too seriously, keep people in your life that can make you laugh ... this work is tiring."

According to Kirkpatrick and Kirkpatrick (2016) there are two types of evaluation inclusive of four levels to evaluating a training program:

- Level 1: Reaction, measures training favorability among participants;
- Level 2: Learning, measures knowledge change;
- Level 3: Behavior, measures application post-training;
- Level 4: Results, measures the degree of targeted outcomes post-training

While the K.A.P.S. workshop only evaluates Level 1 and Level 2 out of the original four levels described by Kirkpatrick and Kirkpatrick (2016) there is opportunity for coordinators to expand into Levels 3 and 4.

UNDERSTANDING THE DATA

The purpose of *Understanding the Data* is to enable the evaluator to determine which statistical tests should be used to analyze the data. The more the evaluator knows about the data, the easier the statistical analysis will be to perform. For many coordinators, the next section of this chapter may be a little daunting, specifically for those who may not like data analysis. However, we have simplified this section into an easy step-by-step process that will hopefully make the data analysis process less daunting.

The first step in the data analysis process is to *Understand the Data*. The evaluator should use the questions and answers in Figure 7.4 to understand the components of the K.A.P.S. data.

Questions to Ask to Understand the Data	Answers from the K.A.P.S Data
Who is your unit of analysis?	Workshop participants
What is the independent variable?	Workshop
What is the dependent variable?	Knowledge
How many participants does the study have?	n = 32
Is the data qualitative or quantitative?	Quantitative: precise close-ended questions that collect both nominal and ordinal data
What are the data sources for this study?	pre- and post-workshop survey questionnaires
Is the data binary or ordinal (Likert)?	Binary (yes/no): used to analyze participants' knowledge and preparedness pre- and post-workshop. Likert (scale 1–5): used to analyze participants' concerns and feelings toward disasters.
What makes the data unique?	The data distribution will most likely be heavily skewed left or right. A statistical test that can account for this distribution is needed; the test should not require a normal distribution.

FIGURE 7.4 Understanding the components of K.A.P.S. data

PREPARING THE DATA

The next step in evaluating the K.A.P.S. training program is to prepare the data. There are three steps to preparing the data for analysis:

1. Type or import all survey data into a statistical program like SPSS or MS Excel.
2. Quality check the document to ensure it is free of errors and mistakes.
3. Begin coding the data according to the steps in Figure 7.4.

Question Type	Ranking Scale with Coded Values
Effective	(1) Not (2) Somewhat (3) Average (4) Very (5) Extremely
Clarity of Workshop	(1) Not (2) Somewhat (3) Average (4) Very (5) Extremely
Interest	(1) Not (2) Somewhat (3) Average (4) Very (5) Extremely
Helpfulness	(1) Not (2) Somewhat (3) Average (4) Very (5) Extremely
Presentation Quality	(1) Not (2) Somewhat (3) Average (4) Very (5) Extremely
Knowledge	(1) No (2) Yes
Preparedness	(1) No (2) Yes
Concerns	(1) Not (2) Somewhat (3) Average (4) Very (5) Extremely
Feelings	(1) Not (2) Somewhat (3) Average (4) Very (5) Extremely

FIGURE 7.5 Rankings used to evaluate K.A.P.S. workshops

As shown in Figure 7.5, K.A.P.S. data contains both Likert scale data (having an ordinal scale of 1–5) and binary data, having dichotomous yes/no options. The binary data can be coded 1 for No and 2 for Yes, while Likert scale data can be coded based on participants' indicated responses on a scale of 1–5 (Babbie, 2013). While there are many statistical tests that can be conducted to analyze the survey data that is collected, this section will describe the test used in the original K.A.P.S. study.

ANALYZING THE DATA

After the data has been prepared, the next step is to analyze the data by using a series of bivariate analyses (Babbie, 2013; Karanci et al., 2005). Conducting bivariate analysis allows the evaluator to quickly assess the association of before and after change per the following hypothesis:

> *Sample Hypothesis:* The participants will experience a change in knowledge as a result of participating in the workshop.

Assessing Binary Data with the McNemar Test

Descriptive statistics and the nonparametric McNemar test were used to analyze the binary data. Descriptive statistics quantitively summarizes the data in terms of mean, median, mode, standard deviation, variance, and other descriptive statistics. The non-parametric McNemar test quantitatively measures data that is not normally distributed to determine differences in dichotomous and categorical variables. It is important to note that when choosing a statistical test, the data needs to meet certain assumptions to ensure accuracy and validity. The four assumptions for performing the McNemar test are found in Figure 7.6 along with

Questions to Ask Before Analyzing	Type of Test	Description
What statistical test should I use to analyze the data?	*Descriptive Statistics:*	Used to summarize participant responses
	McNemar Test:	Determines if differences in binary data are significant
	T-test:	Determines if the mean of the sample's pre-test differs from the means of the sample's post-test
What assumptions should I check before performing the statistical test?	*Descriptive Statistics:*	None
	McNemar Test	1. The data must consist of one categorical dichotomous dependent variable and one categorical independent variable with two related groups
		2. Mutually exclusive
		3. A random sample
	T-test	1. The dependent variable must be continuous
		2. The independent variable should be matched pairs
		3. There are no outliers in the difference between the groups
		4. The distribution of differences should be approximately normally distributed
Are there any exceptions to meeting these assumptions?	*Descriptive Statistics:*	None
	McNemar Test:	Does not require a random sample if conducting field research if all other assumptions are met
	T-test:	Failure to demonstrate a normal distribution and have continuous data can be justified given the robustness of the test

FIGURE 7.6 Questions to ask before analyzing KAPS data.

Source: Laerd Statistics (n.d.), De Winter and Dodou (2010).

exceptions. While the data may not meet the assumption for being from a random sample, use of the McNemar test can be justified if the data is the product of field research or, in this case, a field training. The McNemar test is valid for analysis of K.A.P.S. workshops.

Assessing Likert Scale Data with the T-Test

Likert scale data measures participants' concerns and feelings toward disasters and is analyzed using descriptive statistics (as listed above) and a *t*-test. *T*-tests are typically used to determine if the mean of the sample's pre-test differs from the mean of the sample's post-test. This question is similar to what was asked in the McNemar test; however, the *t*-test compares differences in means before and after, while the McNemar test compares differences in yes/no values before and after.

Statisticians have long debated the use of a *t*-test for Likert scale data, arguing that Likert scale data is ordinal (ranked) rather than ratio or interval, resulting in a skewed distribution. However, studies have shown that a *t*-test can be used for assessing data on a 5-point scale. Similar to performing a McNemar test, there are four assumptions that the data needs to meet prior to performing the *t*-test, which can be found in Figure 7.6 along with the exceptions. While the data may not meet assumption one (continuous data) or assumption two (normal distribution), the literature indicates that if the "chance of an erroneous conclusion" is reduced regardless of violation of the assumptions, the *t*-test can still be used (De Winter and Dodou, 2010: 3).

K.A.P.S. DATA ANALYSIS FOR RESEARCHERS

Disaster researchers often conduct more in-depth analysis beyond the McNemar and *t*-tests. Given categorical data, this analysis would typically involve a Chi-Square Goodness of Fit test, which compares the data to a hypothetical distribution of data. The comparison allows researchers to determine, with statistical accuracy, if each question follows an approximately normal distribution and therefore represents the full population. This is useful because it allows the researcher to identify the significant questions, thus increasing the accuracy of the analysis. The steps for carrying out this analysis are explained below.

1. *Do the participant responses represent a valid data set?* To check, calculate the minimum valid sample size per question.

   Equation 1: $minimum\ n = \dfrac{df + 1}{q}$ (7.1)

Where: df = degrees of freedom

    n = sample size

    q = question range

If your sample size is greater than or equal to the minimum sample size, then the data is valid, and you can keep that question.

2. *Do the participant responses exhibit a preference for any particular question/ category?* Use a Chi-Square Goodness of Fit test to compare the data to the chi-square distribution (which is the square of the normal distribution). We do this by examining participants' observed and expected response frequencies for each question, followed by the chi-square test with a Yates correction for small frequencies (<5 responses per question). Set the significance level to p< 0.05 (or to any desired significance).

Equation 2: *Expected Response Frequency* $(e) = \dfrac{n}{(df + 1)}$ (7.2)

Where: df = degrees of freedom

    n = sample size (per question)

Equation 3: Yates corrected chi $-$ square: $\chi^2 = \dfrac{(f_1 - e_1)^2}{e_1} + \dfrac{(f_2 - e_2)^2}{e_2} \ldots$

                         (7.3)

Where: e_1 = expected frequency for question 1

    f_1 = frequency of responses for question

The result of carrying out Equations 2 and 3 is a chi-square (χ^2) number per question, which are compared to χ^2 Critical, which is obtained from a standard chi-square table. If larger than χ^2 critical, then the observed frequencies are significantly different from the expected frequencies, and the distribution of the data exhibits a statistically significant preference for a peak response category (i.e., the peak of a quasi-normal curve which represents an approximately normal distribution). If less than χ^2 critical, then there is no significant difference between expected and observed response frequencies and no preference for any response category; in this case the data does not display a nearly normal distribution. See the example data results table (Table 7.7). These results provide information about the overall character of the data as well as the statistical significance of each individual question. Chi-square results identify the best questions and the most significant findings in the K.A.P.S. data.

The next section analyzes individual participants.

Question	Item Response (n)	Response Choices	Expected Response (e)	Observed Response (o)	%	Chi-Squared Goodness-of-Fit (p=0.05)			
						df	χ^2	$\chi^2_{critical}$	Significant Result? (Reject H_0)
How responsive do you feel the local and national government organizations will be in addressing a natural or Human-made disaster in your area?	23	Not	4.6	11	48%	4	11.417	9.488	Yes
		Somewhat	4.6	8	35%				
		Average	4.6	3	13%				
		Very	4.6	0	0%				
		Extremely	4.6	1	4%				
How safe would a disaster preparedness plan make you feel?	20	Not	4	3	15%	4	0.250	9.488	No
		Somewhat	4	4	20%				
		Average	4	4	20%				
		Very	4	5	25%				
		Extremely	4	4	20%				
Do you have nonperishable food readily available?	41	Yes	19	33	87%	1	54.72	3.841	Yes
		No	19	5	13%				

FIGURE 7.7 Example chi-square results table

K.A.P.S. DISASTER PREPAREDNESS GROWTH INDEX FOR PRACTITIONERS AND COMMUNITY LEADERS

The statistical analysis presented above is not necessary in many situations. Practitioners and community leaders often want easy-to-use methods for analyzing data that allow them to communicate meaningful information to the broad public. There are two steps for practitioners and community leaders to take in developing a K.A.P.S. Disaster Preparedness Growth Index. First, the practitioner or community leader should convert each individual's survey responses to the same scale. Our recommendation is to use a scale of 0 to 5 per question. A score of 5 indicates that there is a good level of knowledge while a score of 0 indicates that there is no knowledge. The maximum score on the 31-question test is 155.

Binary questions, those that are Yes or No, should be converted using the following scoring metrics:

Yes = 5
No = 0

Likert scale questions do not need conversion, as they are already on a 5-point scale.

Second, the practitioner or community leader should calculate the total score for each participant by adding all the questions to find the simple average. The practitioner or community leader should calculate the simple average for the pre-test and post-test independently, and then find the differences to estimate the growth index.

$$\textbf{Equation 1: } \text{Pre} - \text{test total score} = \left[\frac{Q1 + Q2 + Q3\ldots\ldots Q31}{155} \right] \times 100 \quad (7.4)$$

Where: Q = Question

$$\textbf{Equation 2: } \text{Post} - \text{test total score} = \left[\frac{Q1 + Q2 + Q3\ldots\ldots Q31}{155} \right] \times 100 \quad (7.5)$$

$$\textbf{Equation 3: } \text{Growth Index} = (\text{Post Test Score} - \text{Pre Test Score}) \quad (7.6)$$

PRESENTING THE DATA FOR THE K.A.P.S. DISASTER PREPAREDNESS GROWTH INDEX

After calculating the growth scores, there are three ways that we recommend presenting the data:

1. Announce an Aggregated Growth Index

Calculate the mean growth score by taking the average of all participant scores. Practitioners and community leaders may then announce (verbally or in writing) aggregated scores by saying, for example:

> Prior to participating in the training course, the average participant scored a 50% on the pre-test. After participating in the training course, the average participant scored an 85% on the post-test. The difference between the two scores was 35%, indicating an average growth index of 35%.

2. Ranked Table of Before and After Scores

Rank order the participant scores in separate columns for the pre- and post-test, and difference (growth). Rank ordering participants can help the practitioners and community leaders visually depict the lowest to the highest scores for pre-test, post-test, and growth. Rank ordering can also help the practitioner or community leader calculate individual growth (difference between the scores), which indicates the change in knowledge.

Participant	Pre-test Scores	Post-test Scores	Difference
A	10%	40%	30%
B	30%	50%	20%
C	50%	60%	10%

FIGURE 7.8 Example of rank ordered participant scores

3. Change in Knowledge Graph

Participant pre-test and post-test scores can also be graphed to show a visual depiction of the change in knowledge that occurred because of participating in the K.A.P.S. workshop.

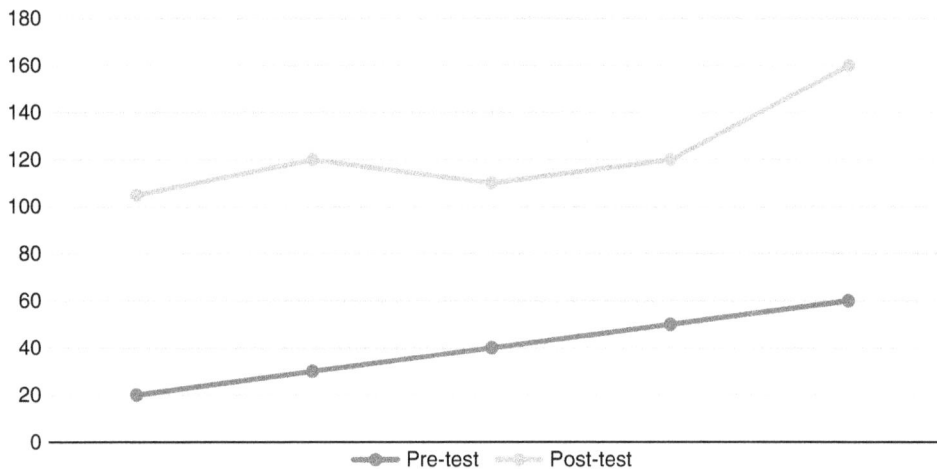

FIGURE 7.9 Change in knowledge for five participants

ENSURING RELIABILITY AND VALIDITY

The final step in evaluating a K.A.P.S. workshop is to ensure that the data is reliable and valid. It is important to protect participants' anonymity and confidentiality. To do so ensure that all data that is collected, prepared, and analyzed is kept confidential. Methods to ensure that data is kept safe can include:

1. Pre-coded questionnaires that do not connect participants by their names
2. Keep physical survey data under lock and key
3. Keep electronic data secure using encryptions and passcodes

Assessing the reliability and validity of the data from the training can ensure quality results. Reliable and valid results can then be used to leverage future fiscal and physical support for stakeholders. The development and implementation of the

K.A.P.S. training uses a mixed method approach that embodies both qualitative and quantitative data collection and analysis increasing the reliability and validity of the data (Babbie, 2013: 188). While the results from the training program cannot be generalized to an entire community because it uses a non-probability combination of a self-selection, snowball, and convenience sampling method to attract participants, it can serve as an exploratory pilot study that can be leveraged to argue the need for additional community specific trainings.

The reliability of the data from the training is increased by taking two (2) surveys (pre- and post-) that contain several questions asked multiple times in different forms to ensure reliability of the participant answers (Babbie, 2013). While evaluators can choose to add additional questions to their own surveys, the survey questions presented in this book are peer-reviewed and validated. If evaluators would like to add additional questions and/or change the workshop, any changes should be field tested to ensure clarity, consistency, and reliability (Babbie, 2013). Preliminary field tests can vet any changes to ensure that the workshop is clear, free of errors, and progresses in a timely manner. Reliability and validity of the workshop increases as the facilitator and the evaluator incorporate secondary data such as like from Census.gov, American Fact Finder, and parish/state/federal government websites. Literature reviews that examine best practices for emergency management can also increase validity.

CHAPTER 8

Afterword

Socially vulnerable communities, specifically those of color and/or of low income, often disproportionately experience hazards in intensity, frequency, and duration (Bolin and Kurtz, 2018; Bolin and Bolton, 1986). As a result, these communities often have a difficult time proceeding through the disaster cycle (mitigating, preparing, responding, and recovering) (Schwab et al., 1998; Fothergill et al., 1999). The inability to effectively proceed through the disaster cycle reflects their susceptibility to the loss of life and property.

One method to increase a community's capacity to mitigate, prepare, respond, and recover from disastrous impacts is through disaster education, which is the central focus of this book (Muttarak and Lutz, 2014). Disaster education, in this sense, can then be used to increase a resident's Knowledge, Attitude, Preparedness, and Skills (K.A.P.S.) toward disastrous impacts. Though we recognize that disaster education is not a complete solution for dealing with the disproportionalities that exist within socially vulnerable communities, it can serve as a steppingstone to increase the capacity of the community to effectively proceed through the disaster cycle (Semien and Nance, 2019).

The main purpose of this handbook is to provide researchers, practitioners, and community leaders with a set of practical instructional tools that can be used to increase K.A.P.S. among vulnerable populations. This book uses a bottom-up training approach to ensure trainers know how to build awareness and empower community members to prepare for a disaster. While the case-study training course took place originally in Geismar, Louisiana the workshop lesson plans and evaluation metrices can be used to increase K.A.P.S. within other communities.

DOI: 10.4324/9781003177005-11

APPENDIX A

Lesson Plans

....

LESSON PLAN EXAMPLE

Knowledge in K.A.P.S.

Introduction

Disasters are often one of the most sudden and unexpected challenges a family can go through. But if you are prepared, the stress associated with the issues that arise can be somewhat alleviated.

Definition

> A disaster is an incident that causes damage to human lives, infrastructure, the environment, and the economy because of a natural or manmade event.
> National Red Cross and Red Crescent Federation

Key Information about Disasters

- Disasters are sporadic—they happen with little to no notice at the most inconvenient times. Statistics show that disasters are becoming increasingly frequent and powerful.
- Sometimes we take for granted the structures and systems that are there to protect us. We assume that these structures will always do their job, but these structures are human-made and have tendencies to fail which is why it is important to always be prepared!

There are many types of disasters, broken into two categories: **Natural** and **Human-Made.**

- **Natural:** Flood, Fire, Tornado, Windstorm, Wildfires, Droughts, Earthquakes, and Hail.
- **Human-Made:** Industrial Explosion, Chemical Leak, Oil Spill, Fire, and Blackout.

LESSON PLAN EXAMPLE

Knowledge in K.A.P.S.

Definition

Vulnerability is the weakness, that you and/or your family may possess that can increase your risk of injury or damage. Having a high rate of vulnerability places you at a higher risk of being impacted by a disaster.

What Makes You Vulnerable?

- **Proximity to the Coast**
  Every year Louisiana Coast experiences various hurricanes and other tropical systems due to its proximity to the Gulf of Mexico and the Atlantic Ocean. As a result, these storms place many residents at risk for damages and fatalities.
- **Position in the Industrial Corridor**
  The industrial corridor or Cancer Alley stretches 85 miles containing 100 chemical plants, releasing 132 pounds of toxins into the air. The toxins place many residents at risk for many health concerns, for example asthma and cancer.
- **Demographics: Who you are**
  o The second issue that makes you more or less vulnerable to the occurrence of disasters is who you are. Elderly, children, and those medically ill or disabled are the groups most vulnerable to the impacts of disasters. These groups have a harder time than the average population because of physical immobility and resources. Minority populations are also another group that is regularly impacted by these disasters because these populations usually live closer to areas of higher vulnerability like the coast, chemical plants, rivers etc. Other factors include education limitations such as disaster trainings/courses and income.

Name	Address	Phone #	Description
St. Elizabeth Hospital	1125 Louisiana 30 W. Gonzales, LA 70737	225-647-5000	Local hospital
Lamar Dixon	9039 S. St Landry Ave Gonzales, La 70737	Check the news for updates	During a storm, an individual can seek shelter here if being utilized.
Donaldsonville High School	100 Tiger Drive Donaldsonville, La	Check the news for updates	During a storm, an individual can seek shelter here if being utilized.
Ascension Parish Counseling Agency	1112 ASE Ascension Complex Blvd. Gonzales, La 70737	225-450-1203	In the case an individual is overwhelmed or stressed before or after a storm they can visit the Counseling Agency for support.
Office of Homeland Security and Emergency Preparedness	828 S. Irma Blvd. Building 3 Gonzales, LA 70737	225-621-8360	Provide information on community preparedness
Community Information Number		1-866-380-2303	
Community Apps	WAFB News App WBRZ.Com News App Code Red Community App		
Other Information	Ascensionparish.net/ohsep www.twitter.com/ascensionohsep www.apsb.org www.facebook.com/apohsep www.twitter.com/asecensionparish		
Television	Ascension Paris Ch 21 WAFB (CBS Channel 9) WBRZ (ABC Channel 20 WVLA (NBC Channel 33) Gonzales & 12 (Donaldsonville)		
Alert Notifications:	Sign up with www.tuinyurl.com/ascensiongov to revieve alerts by phone, app, text, and e-mail. Community Information Line 1-866-380-2303		
Radio	KKAY	AM	1590
	WYNK	FM	101.5
	WFMF	FM	102.5
	KQXL	FM	106.5
	WNXX	FM	104.9

FIGURE A1 Disaster resources for social media release

LESSON PLAN EXAMPLE

Test Your Knowledge in K.A.P.S.

1. _____ are often one of the most sudden and unexpected challenges a family can go through.
2. Give three examples of a natural disaster _____, _____, and _____.
3. Give three examples of a human made disaster _____, _____, and _____.

4. Who you are and where you live increases levels of _____ to disaster impacts?
5. Describe the hazard in the below figure.

FIGURE A2 Image of a playground in front of an industrial plant located in Norco, Louisiana

LESSON PLAN EXAMPLE

Attitude in K.A.P.S.

"A" is the second letter of the acronym K.A.P.S. The letter "A" stands for Attitude! Having the right attitude and perception toward approaching a disaster is everything! If a person believes a storm is approaching than they will prepare for the storm's arrival, however if a person believes the storm is a hoax than they will be less likely to prepare and be at significant risk to acquiring damages.

Why does Attitude Matter?

- In many cases the way a person conceptualizes and perceives a disaster will impact their stress levels.
- There are three areas that play a large part in the survival rate of an individual or family:

o *Misconception:* an incorrect opinion based on flawed thinking and understandings;
o *Perception:* the opinion or belief of an individual based on how a situation appears; and
o *Stress:* the tension an individual experiences because of external stimuli.

Misconception

The first target area to developing a positive attitude towards disasters is breaking all misconceptions.

Approach every disaster well prepared and ready to evacuate at any time. This will increase you and your family's survival rates.

Myth: in the event of a disaster the government will be there immediately to pick up the pieces

Reality: it takes time for the government to deploy necessary resources

LESSON PLAN EXAMPLE

Attitude in K.A.P.S.

Perception

The second target area to developing a positive attitude towards disasters is breaking all false perceptions of a storm's power.

- Never underestimate the power of a storm because a storm's power can change at any time.
- Never completely trust in human-made protective structures like levees to protect you, those things can fail and have been known to fail during a disaster.
  o Example storms: Hurricane Katrina, Rita, Gustav, and Isaac.
- Take precaution beforehand: mitigation actions taken well in advance of disasters will help to avoid or reduce disaster-related damage later.

Many people maintain a false perception of a storm's power. Many people even after the news entities have released warnings regarding storms, dismiss the reality of the **power** of the storm. Many times, especially as a southern resident, we often take for granted the storms that come through because they are frequent and sometimes they are not as powerful as the news entities suggest they will be. Never underestimate the **power** of a storm because it can change at any time.

It is important to understand the types of disasters, the impacts they can cause, and develop a clear perspective on how to act in the case of a disaster. In other words, be prepared for the possibility of a disaster and in the case of a disaster stay tuned to radios/T.V. stations and **Always Stay Off the Phone!**

LESSON PLAN EXAMPLE

Attitude in K.A.P.S.

Stress

The third target that can play a huge part in surviving during a disaster is **stress**. Stress leads to panic, delayed responses, and/or overreaction. **Stress** can be decreased by knowing what to expect, how to respond, and having a strong community network. It is important to seek counseling help after a disaster.

While there are many different techniques that can alleviate stress during a disaster, our favorite is the S.T.O.P. method: when you are in the midst of a disaster and you feel yourself becoming overwhelmed, tensed, or stressed just: **Stop, Think, Organize, and Proceed.**

- **Stop:** Stop talking, stop panicking, and just breathe.
- **Think:** think about the facts and risks related to the upcoming disaster.
- **Organize:** organize your facts and your belongings.
- **Proceed:** to do what you believe is right for you and your family to do.

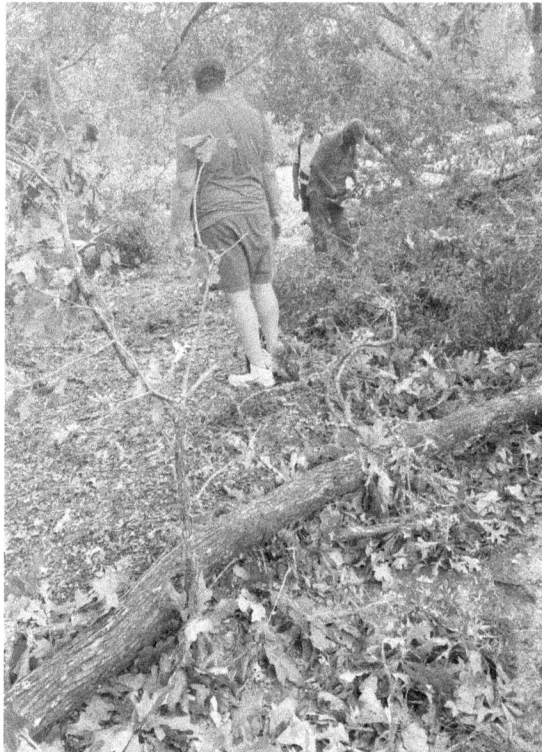

FIGURE A3 Community members cleaning up after 2021 Hurricane Ida

LESSON PLAN EXAMPLE

Attitude in K.A.P.S.

How to Relieve Stress Before a Disaster

- Think about the facts and risks related to the upcoming disasters and decide whether to stay at home or evacuate.
- Tune into local media, download the Ascension Parish CODE RED App to obtain all of the information about the disaster as well as develop a complete understanding of all risks associated with the storm.
- The most important thing when deciding whether or not to stay at home or to evacuate is to understand the risks associated with both as well as to understand the predicted strengths related to the impacts of the storm.
- The first thing you should do before you make this decision is to stay informed. Tune into local media to develop a complete understanding of all risks associated with the storm.

How to Relieve Stress During a Disaster

1. Take slow deep breaths or rapid and shallow breaths (this resets your breathing and relaxes you).
2. You can also try distracting yourself, meditating, praying, self talking, for example saying "I'm Okay right now."
3. You can also try muscle relaxation exercises by tensing your muscles and then relaxing them. This helps you identify where the tension may lie in your body while tightening the muscles can help you relax.

LESSON PLAN EXAMPLE

Attitude in K.A.P.S.

Decide whether to stay home or evacuate

Staying at Home

- Pre-stock cabinets with water, canned goods, toilet paper etc.
- Fill all cars with extra gas
- Fill all bathtubs and other big containers with water
- Fasten down all loose material in and around the home
- Board up and seal all windows and holes to the outside of the home

Evacuate

- Fill all cars with extra gas

- Bring a completed disaster supply kit for each person traveling
- Before leaving, turn off and unplug all appliances except the refrigerator and the freezer
- Clean out the refrigerator and the freezer before you leave
- Lift up all valuable items off of the floors
- Update neighbors, family members of your travel

During a Disaster Don't Wait, Have a Plan, Act Now and Just Proceed

LESSON PLAN EXAMPLE

Test your Attitude in K.A.P.S.

1. The names of the three parish shelters are _____, _____, and _____.
2. Learn to _____ rather than _____.
3. Don't Wait! Act_____!
4. What is the name of the Ascension Parish App used to notify residents of disasters? _____!

FIGURE A4 Damage to a building in south Louisiana after 2020 Hurricanes Laura and Delta

LESSON PLAN EXAMPLE

Preparedness in K.A.P.S.

Before you can prepare for a disaster you must understand that a disaster is possible. They can affect you and your family in a moment's notice. A disaster can happen at any time, and in any place.

What Does it Mean to be Prepared?

Disaster preparedness refers to measures taken to reduce the effects of **disasters**. That is, to predict and, where possible, prevent disasters, mitigate their impact on vulnerable populations.

IFRC

Understanding the types of disasters and how to properly respond can directly increase the level to which you and your family are impacted.

What types of disasters are more prone to affect Geismar, Louisiana?

Due to Geismar's proximity to the coast and its location in the Louisiana industrial corridor there are four types of disasters Geismar is most prone to: **Chemical Emergencies, Hurricanes, Tornados,** and **Flooding.**

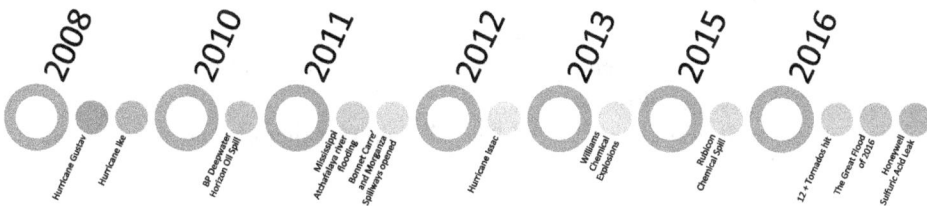

FIGURE A5 Timeline of events impacting Geismar, Louisiana

LESSON PLAN EXAMPLE

Preparedness in K.A.P.S.

What is a Chemical Emergency?

A **chemical emergency** occurs when a hazardous **chemical** has been released [or an explosion has taken place] and the release has the potential for harming people's health.

CDC

How to Respond to a Chemical Emergency

Step 1: Listen for the Sirens

1. Tested every Monday at 12:00 p.m.
2. 26 sirens around the parish
3. Can be heard within a 2.5-mile radius

Step 2: Shelter in Place

1. Go inside the closest building
2. Close and lock all the doors and windows (use tape to seal windows and other holes)
3. Place a towel under the windows and doors
4. Turn off all fans, air conditioners, and heaters
5. Turn on the T.V. and listen to the phone: "First Call" may be activated to alert residents of spills, explosions etc.
6. Stay inside until you hear the "All Clear" siren or otherwise notified via phone, radio, T.V., etc.

LESSON PLAN EXAMPLE

Test your Preparedness in K.A.P.S.

What is a Hurricane?

A hurricane is a type of storm called a tropical cyclone, which forms over tropical or subtropical waters.

NOAA

Hurricanes are usually not named "hurricanes" until they reach 74 mph. At this point the max winds of the hurricane is than rated on a **Saffir-Simpson Hurricane Wind Scale** and given a rating of **1 to 5**.

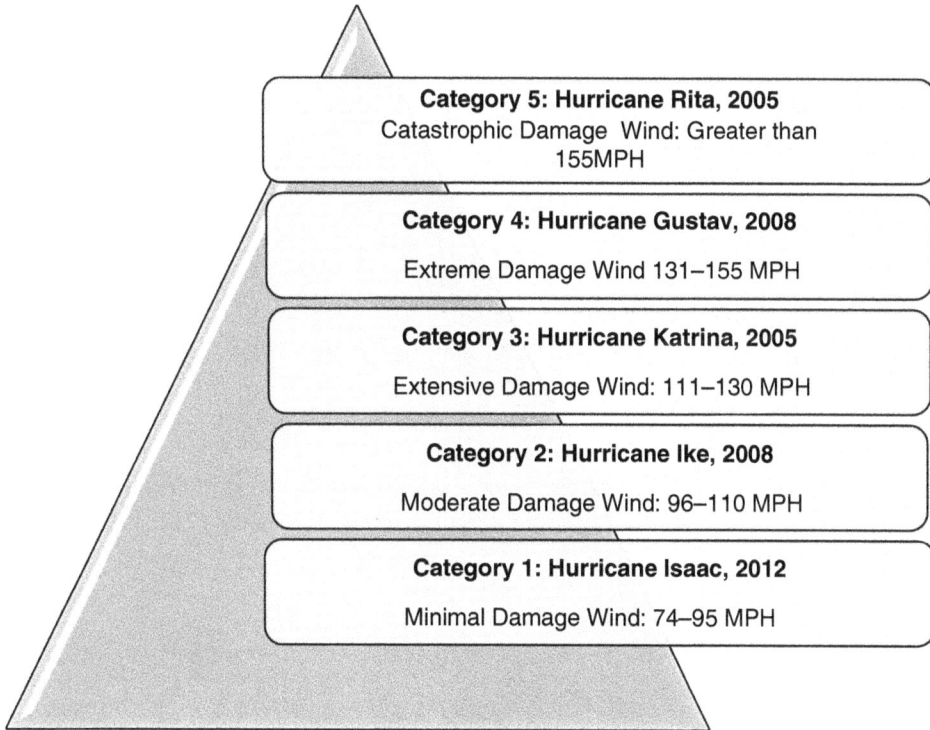

FIGURE A6 Image depicting the Hurricane Categories with example storms impacting Geismar, Louisiana

Preparing for a Hurricane

The task of preparing for a hurricane is something every family living in Southeast Louisiana should do. Being prepared is the key to survival. Know that **Hurricane Season** begins **June 1** and stretches to **November 30**. It is important to stay up to date with developing storms. Families can visit websites like these www.weather.gov, www.NOAA.gov, www.wbrz.com, or www.wafb.com to stay up to date. These outlets will provide you with the information needed to decide whether you and your family should **stay at home** or **evacuate**.

LESSON PLAN EXAMPLE

Test your Preparedness in K.A.P.S.

What is a Tornado?

A tornado is a narrow, violently rotating column of air that extends from the base of a thunderstorm to the ground.

NOAA

How to Respond to a Tornado

Tornados are extremely dangerous since they are so sporadic. The best thing you can do for you and your family is to be prepared and know how to properly respond to the occurrence of a tornado.

Important Facts About Hurricanes

- Gulf Coast tornado Season is **May to June**
- If in a **car, GET OUT** and take shelter in a building or a low-lying area
- If in a **mobile home, GET OUT** and take shelter in a building that has a sturdy foundation
- If in a home with a cement foundation **go into a room with no windows** (hallway or closet) or the lowest area of the home.
  - o Place a mattress over you or another durable piece of furniture to resist debris
  - o Crouch down on your knees and protect your head with your arms

FIGURE A7 Damage to building in south Louisiana after 2021 Hurricane Ida

LESSON PLAN EXAMPLE

Test your Preparedness in K.A.P.S.

What is Flooding

Flooding is an overflowing of water onto land that is normally dry.

NOAA

Flash floods are extremely harmful since they are fast and "unpredictable". Usually, the result of water filling creeks, riverbeds at a fast pace without warning.

Flooding is quite common for Ascension Parish and during the recent flood in August, 2016 Geismar experienced large amounts of unregular flooding. This is due to the many low-lying areas and ditches that are usually filled with debris, as a result the water cannot flow causing widespread flooding.

How to Respond to Flooding

- Always check the T.V. or radio for flooding information
- Decide whether to stay at home or to evacuate (If not mandatory)
- Make sure mobile or loose items are bolted to the ground
- Elevate all valuables
- Collect sandbags to place around homes
- Leave during daylight and check evacuation routes

How to Return Home After Flooding

- Wear protective clothing, for example gloves, long sleeves, open toe shoes, pants
- Check for damage to home before entering
- Do not use an open flame for light
- Check food for spoilage and don't drink the tap water
- Visit home during daylight hours and check the evacuation routes for road closures before visiting.

LESSON PLAN EXAMPLE

Test your Preparedness in K.A.P.S.

1. It is important for you and your family to _____ for a disaster.
2. What are the four types of disasters that can affect you, your family and the Geismar community discussed throughout this section of the workshop?
   1. _____, 2._____, 3. _____, and 4. _____.
3. If you must evacuate leave during _____ hours and check _____ routes.

FIGURE A8 Image of a down powerline in south Louisiana after 2021 Hurricane Ida

LESSON PLAN EXAMPLE

Skills in K.A.P.S.

How do you Adequately Prepare for a Disaster?

1. Design a Plan
2. Practice Your Plan
3. Build a Disaster Preparedness Kit
4. Practice your Disaster Preparedness Kit

Design a Family Plan

- Make a list of emergency contacts
- Make a list of family members
- Make a list of pet information
- Make a copy identification cards, and medical info.
- Make a copy of all insurance papers (car, house etc.)
- Determine the best routes to escape from your home
- Find the safe spots in or near your home for every type of disaster

* Establish two meeting places outside the home and away from the home
* Establish a family contact within the state and out of the state

LESSON PLAN EXAMPLE

Skills in K.A.P.S.

What to Include in a Disaster Preparedness Kit

* Backpack
* Family Plan
* Pens/Markers
* Flashlight
* Battery Packs
* Radio
* Candles
* Matches
* Manuel Can Opener
* Non-perishable Food
* Energy Foods/Crackers
* Plastics Utensils
* 1 Gallon Water
* Water Purification Tablets
* First Aid Kit
* Band-Aids
* Antibacterial Ointments
* Toiletries
* Toothbrush
* Toothpaste
* Shampoo
* Conditioner
* Soap
* Deodorant
* Feminine Hygiene Products
* Comb/Brush
* Medications
* Portable Chargers
* Disposable Camera
* Hand Sanitizer
* Toilet Paper
* Towels
* Sunscreen
* Bug Spray

- Garbage Bags
- Zip-lock Bags
- Small Tool Kit
- Pocket Knife
- Small Screwdriver
- Scissors
- Whistle
- Duct Tape
- Lysol Wipes to go
- Small Notebook
- Umbrella
- Raincoat
- Particle Respirator
- Blankets/Pillows/Sleeping Bags
- Cash & Quarters
- Pet Supplies
- Gloves
- Toys for kids
- Glasses
- Diapers & Baby Wipes
- Keys

LESSON PLAN EXAMPLE

Skills in K.A.P.S.

Types of Identification

- License or State ID
- Social Security Card
- Birth Certificates
- Passport
- Visa/Green Card/Permanent Residence Card
- Military Discharge Document

Other Important Documents

- Vehicle Registration
- Vehicle Title
- Marriage License
- Medical Information
- Monthly Bills
- Bank Account
- Insurance (Home/car)

- House Note
- Rent Information
- Emergency Contact Card

LESSON PLAN EXAMPLE

Skills in K.A.P.S.

Pet Supplies and Important Documents

- Adoption records
- Vaccination records
- Health records
- Veterinarian information
- Toys
- Carrying case
- Extra food, water, leash, and pet carrier

LESSON PLAN EXAMPLE

Skills in K.A.P.S.

Medical Information

Patient Name	Doctors Name/Phone Number	Medication Name	Pharmacy Name/Number

FIGURE A9 Medical information chart

Medical Documents

- Insurance Card
- Medicaid/Medicare Card
- Prescription
- Medicines

- Immunizations Records
- Disability Documents
- Medical Equipment

LESSON PLAN EXAMPLE

Let's Practice the Skills in K.A.P.S.

Scenario

It's 2 o'clock in the morning. You hear someone banging on the door. As you rise out of bed to see who it could possibly be, you realize that the floor is damp. Not thinking twice about it, you continue to the front door. The closer you get to the door you realize it's your neighbor. So out of confusion and concern you open the door only to be met by rushing water as it rapidly enters your house. You look up and your neighbor is screaming "We have to get out now!"

What would you do next?

1. What **type of disaster** is your scenario? _____
2. Is this a **human made** or **natural disaster?** _____
3. How would you **react** to this scenario? Why?

   _____

   _____
4. How would you **respond** to this scenario? Why?

   _____

   _____
5. Do you **evacuate** or do you **stay at home?** _____
6. What **items within your box** would you use to solve this scenario? Why?

   _____

   _____
7. Name ways to **stay calm** during this scenario.

   _____

   _____

LESSON PLAN EXAMPLE

Let's Practice the Skills in K.A.P.S.

Scenario

It's 4 o'clock in the afternoon, and you are on your way home from work. You decided to take the long way home because it's such a beautiful day. Halfway home the sky starts to turn gray, and you suddenly realize that this was a bad idea. The closer you get home the more the sky darkens, and the rain begins to pour. By the time you get home the sky is black and the rain is so thick you can't see the front door. Once in the house you immediately turn on the T.V. to find a weather alert for a tornado warning! What would you do next?

1. What type of disaster is your scenario? _____
2. Is this a human made or natural disaster? _____
3. How would you **react** to this scenario? Why?

   _____

   _____

4. How would you **respond** to this scenario? Why?

   _____

   _____

5. Do you **evacuate** or do you **stay at home**? _____
6. What **items within your box** would you use to solve this scenario? Why?

   _____

   _____

7. Name ways to **stay calm** during this scenario.

   _____

   _____

LESSON PLAN EXAMPLE

Let's Practice the Skills in K.A.P.S.

Scenario

It's Friday afternoon and you just got home from a long vacation in Paris, Texas. You decide to call a friend and watch T.V. as you begin to unpack your suitcase. While unpacking and talking, you hear the weather guy announce that a category 4 hurricane has formed in the Gulf of Mexico, it will reach landfall in 8 hours and head directly towards you. What would you do?

1. What type of disaster is your scenario? _____
2. Is this a human made or natural disaster? _____
3. How would you **react** to this scenario? Why?

   _____

   _____

4. How would you **respond** to this scenario? Why?

   _____

   _____

5. Do you **evacuate** or do you **stay at home**? _____

6. What **items within your box** would you use to solve this scenario? Why?

   _____

   _____

7. Name ways to **stay calm** during this scenario.

   _____

   _____

LESSON PLAN EXAMPLE

Let's Practice the Skills in K.A.P.S.

Scenario

Its Saturday morning and you just woke up. You decided to fix yourself pancakes for breakfast. In the middle of the third pancake, you hear the chemical siren going off; alerting you that there is a chemical emergency. What would you do?

1. What type of disaster is your scenario? _____
2. Is this a human made or natural disaster? _____
3. How would you **react** to this scenario? Why?

   _____

   _____

4. How would you **respond** to this scenario? Why?

   _____

   _____

5. Do you **evacuate** or do you **stay at home**? _____
6. What **items within your box** would you use to solve this scenario? Why?

   _____

   _____

7. Name ways to **stay calm** during this scenario.

   _____

   _____

Materials to Build a K.A.P.S. Community Training

....

developing a railroad station along the river. The entrepreneurship made way for a post office, a General Store, boarding house, and two schools to separately house both black and white children. By the early 1930s the country had entered into a Great Depression causing the partnership to go into bankruptcy. During this time the railroad station shrank, the boarding house was closed, and the Waterloo plantation burned down which officially marked the "end of an era." By the late 1950s, chemical companies began to take root within the area aiding in the rise of the great "Mississippi Chemical Corridor" otherwise known as "Cancer Alley". Today Geismar is home to approximately 7,754 residents as well as 18 chemical plants—the prime sources of taxable revenue within the community (Census, 2010; Wright, 2009). Geismar still maintains an unwritten segregation law where African Americans live predominately closer to the river and Caucasians, as well as other races, live further away from the river.

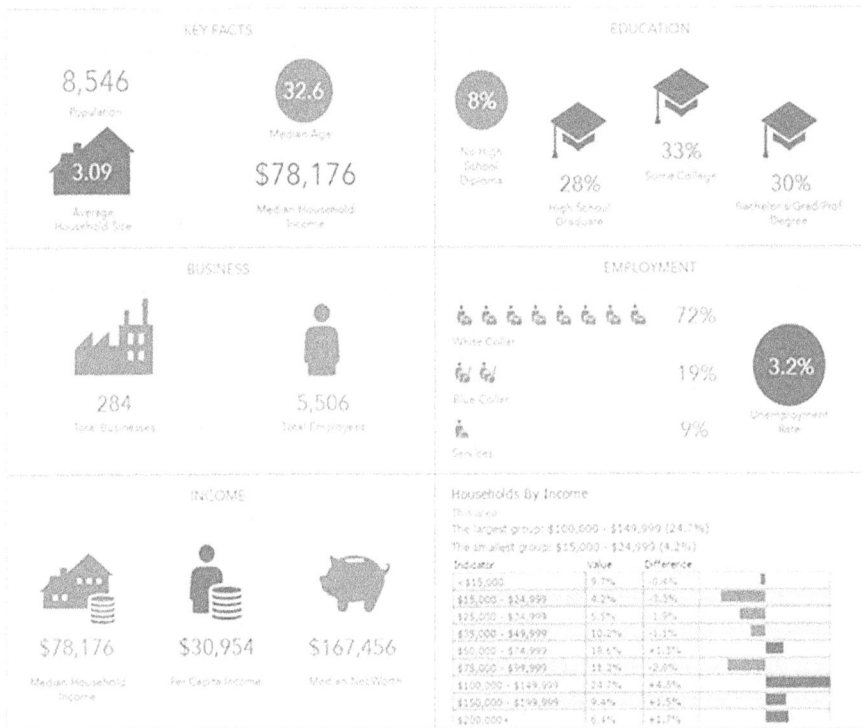

FIGURE B1 Community Profile Diagram

Geographic/Topographical Layout

The 10-square-mile region of Geismar, Louisiana is in the parish of Ascension. This geographically unique unincorporated community borders the Mississippi

River and is approximately 200 miles from the Louisiana Gulf Coast, increasing the area's susceptibility to hurricanes, tornadoes, and other tropical systems. In the past, the area was known for its rich soil for farming sugar cane and other crops but today the area is populated with over 18 chemical plants that discharge approximately 200 million pounds of toxic emissions into the air, soil, and water each year (Wright, 2009). As a result, farming and fishing in this community is limited due to the toxicity of the soil and water. Many of these challenges can be seen in bordering towns like St. Gabriel, Carville, Sunshine, Donaldsonville, Gonzales, Prairieville, and Darrow, who all are former plantation communities heavily comprised of slave descendants.

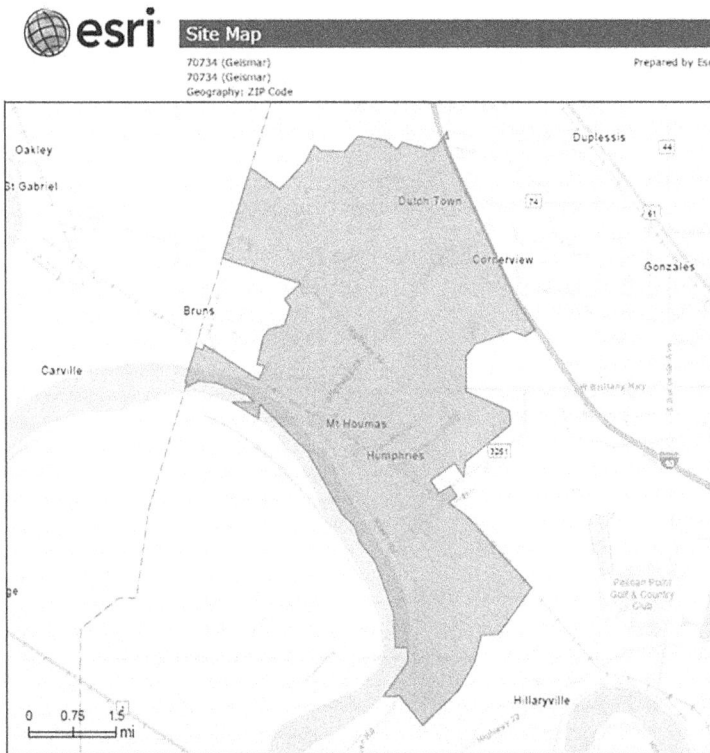

FIGURE B2 Map of Geismar

Population Assessment

Population statistics were collected from the 2010 U.S. Census. Zip code 70734 was used to gather the information. The Census showed the population in 2010 to be 7,754, having a vulnerable population of 619 elderly people over the age of 60, and 2,718 children under the age of 18 (Census, 2010). Geismar has a population demographic that predominately consists of White/Caucasian and African Americans. Geismar has a predominately white population of 68.3 percent living away from the river and 27.7 percent black population living closer to the river (Census, 2010; Wright, 2009).

Year	Ascension Parish	Geismar, LA Zip Code: 70734	Plausible Reason for Population Impacts
1830	5,426		Later part of the industrial revolution
1840	6,951		First wave of immigration
1850	10,752		
1860	11,484		Civil War
			Homestead Act/Morrill Act passed /
1870	11,677		Housing reform, sanitary, open space, railroad built
1880	16,895		Second wave of immigration
1890	19,895		City beautiful
1900	24,142		
1910	23,837		World War I
1920	22,155		Women's Suffrage,
1930	19,996		Great Depression,
1940	21,215		World War II
1950	22,387		Civil Rights
1960	27,927		Chemical companies move into the area
1970	37,086		Integration of Louisiana Public Schools, Universities,
1980	50,068		Public occupations
1990	58,214		
2000	76,627	3,324	Hurricane Katrina
2010	107,215	7,617	(Newest waves of immigration)

FIGURE B3 Geismar and Ascension Parish Population Data

Source: Census.gov and American Fact Finder.

Political

After several failed attempts at incorporation, Geismar remains an unincorporated community governed by the parish laws of Ascension Parish. The community follows the government structure of the Parish of Ascension within the state of Louisiana. The Parish has its own governing system consisting of a Parish President and a host of council members that are from various parts of the Parish. The team meets monthly to discuss the Parish budgets and other issues arising across the Parish. In addition, the Parish Council supports several working offices such as the Planning and Zoning, Public Works, Health and Wellness, Security and Emergency, and the Sheriff Department.

Economic

The biggest source of jobs for the community are small to medium size businesses like grocery stores, glass shops, auto shops, schools, and daycares. While the community has a high population of chemical plants many of those jobs are outsourced to people living outside of the community. Many residents leave the parish for employment as the community has a high career specialization whose jobs cannot be found within the local community.

Housing

Over the last 10 years, the housing prices have increased rapidly due to the increasing expectation of population increase, the development of new business, and schools. Today there are approximately 2,451 households in Geismar maintaining an average family income of approximately $74,898.00 (Census, 2010). Of the 2,451 households, 487 households are renter occupied while the remaining are owner-occupied.

Transportation

While there are no public transportation services available in the community, there are two major thruways: Interstate-10, Highway 73, and Highway 30 which connects the community to the metropolitan areas of Baton Rouge, La and New Orleans, La as well as other bordering towns. Highway 30 is the main transportation route that allows industrial plants to transport material throughout the community.

Community Infrastructure

The community is home to the "Jackie Robinson Memorial Park" maintained by the Parish of Ascension. The heavily delipidated park contains minimal recreational equipment and a large baseball field used competitively for games. Geismar is also home to the Richard Brown Community Center initially designed to house community activities like after school programs and summer camps. Today the center is typically booked out for individual social events to anyone in the parish but can be used for other events if booked in advance (approximately 2–3 months). The community currently has four schools, Spanish Lake Primary, Dutchtown Primary, Dutchtown Middle, and Dutchtown High School. The community also has a local library run by the Parish of Ascension located across from the local schools. There is one volunteer fire department in the community that operates through parish funding and donations.

Disaster, Environmental and Health Impact Analysis

In the late 1950s, chemical companies began to take root within the area aiding in the rise of the great "Mississippi Chemical Corridor" otherwise known as "Cancer Alley" (Bullard and Johnson, 2000). "Industrial waste facilities producing hazardous waste and excessive amounts of pollution … are often located in areas with low property values because of the economic advantages of locating there" (Lambert, 2013: 206; Nance, 2009: 293). As a result of this economic imbalance many African slave descendants' families were directly affected by the influx of Chemical Plants along the river. As many families were severely affected with many adverse health effects associated with the pollutants released by the chemical plants found within the community. Today Geismar sits in the middle of the Mississippi River Chemical Corridor, an 85-mile stretch of 135 petrochemical plants from Baton Rouge to New Orleans, Louisiana. Every year the corridor spews out hundreds of thousands of pounds of pollutants into the air and water (Wright, 2009). The chemical plants within this region collectively discharge approximately 250 million pounds of toxic emissions into the air, soil, and water each year (U.S. EPA, 2021; Reed 1991; Wright, 2009).

This particular area is also vulnerable to hurricanes, tornadoes and other tropical systems due to the geographical proximity within southeast Louisiana. Over the last several decades the area has been experiencing increased rates at which it is affected by both natural and anthropogenic disturbances (Bullard, 2000). As a result of the amount of yearly discharge released each year from the petrochemical plants and the frequency of natural disasters the area develops a higher rate of vulnerability increasing the risk for loss of life or property (Cutter et al., 2003). As a result of these compound events, the parish maintains a host of community emergency alerting systems such as chemical sirens, phone apps, radio stations, and conducts periodic workshops throughout the parish. One of the biggest problems in the community is that although the information is periodically given out, very few workshops are held in the community of Geismar, and thousands of people go untrained each year.

Conclusion

Every year Geismar is faced with the risk of both natural and human made disasters such as hurricanes, tornados, flooding, chemical leaks, and industrial explosions which has a direct impact on the high vulnerability level of its residents. In implementing the K.A.P.S. workshop the training material should focus on synthesizing commonly used practices and adapting those practices to the Geismar community to develop the best possible lesson plans to encourage participant engagement within the community. The main goal of this workshop is to increase disaster preparedness knowledge levels across the community.

APPENDIX BOX B2 EXAMPLE: STAKEHOLDER ASSESSMENT

Stakeholders Name: _____ Organization Name: _____

1. Identify type of Stakeholder (Select One):
   o Local
   o Regional
   o National
   o International
2. Have you ever worked with the community of _____?
   o Yes
   o No
3. If so, how long did you work with the community of _____?
4. Identify type of Stakeholder (Select One):
   o Church Leader
   o Nonprofit Organization
   o Business Owner
   o Practitioner
   o Politician
   o Researcher
5. How long have you worked in this capacity? _____
6. Have you ever performed or implemented activities that supported the community's capacity to proceed throughout the emergency management cycle? If so, describe your role and experience.

   _____

   What were some of your achievements from your past experiences working with the community? _____
7. What were some of your challenges from your past experiences working with the community?

   _____

8. What are some of the supplies and resources that from your experience, every community member should have within their household? _____

   _____

9. What are some of the major disaster impacts that the community has seen?"

   _____

10. What disaster mitigation strategies and preparedness concepts still need to be assessed when collaborating with this community? _____
11. Are you aware of any past disaster preparedness resources provided to this community in the past, for example disaster preparedness kits, supplies etc.? _____

APPENDIX BOX B3 EXAMPLE: LETTER TO REQUEST COMMUNITY STAKEHOLDER PARTICIPATION

The KAPS Team
1234 KAPS Rd.
Houston, TX 12345

Date: October 16, 2016
Subject: Request for Stakeholder Participation

To Whom it may concern:

Natural and human-made disasters are increasing in both intensity and in duration. Every year we see growth in both natural and human-made disasters like oil spills, tropical storms, hurricanes, and wildfires. Every disaster that hits our state brings increased risk of loss of life and property. To reduce this risk, there is a need for disaster preparedness training to build community awareness, preparation, and empowerment.

We are currently looking for stakeholder participation to partner with us to spread disaster preparedness information to the community, recruit community members, and/or supply disaster related resources. Your partnership will help to empower and engage the community of Geismar, Louisiana in preparing for a possible disaster related event.

If you are interested in becoming a stakeholder, please contact _____ by phone or e-mail at KAPSdisastertraining@gmail.com.

Thank you in advance for your commitment a participation in the project.

Sincerely,
The KAPS Team

APPENDIX BOX B4 EXAMPLE: LETTER TO REQUEST FISCAL SUPPORT

> The K.A.P.S. Team
> 1234 K.A.P.S. Rd.
> Houston, TX 12345

Date: October 16, 2016
Subject: Request for Stakeholder Participation
Subject: K.A.P.S. Disaster Workshop – Donations Request
To: Geismar Business

In Louisiana, both natural and human-made disasters are quite prevalent as evidenced by increasing tropical storms, hurricanes, and oil spills. Every disaster that hits our state brings increased risk of loss of life and property. To reduce this risk, there is a need for disaster preparedness training to build community awareness, preparation, and empowerment. My name is Joy Semien, I am a member of the K.A.P.S. disaster training team, we will be holding two disaster preparedness workshops in Geismar during the 2016 hurricane season (Fall of 2016). By way of this letter, I am requesting assistance from local organizations and individuals so that participants of the workshop will have the supplies necessary to build their own disaster preparedness kits for use during natural or man-made disasters. My goal is to acquire enough supplies for 60 participants.

To ensure the success of the workshop, I am reaching out to you and your business to request your support either in the form of a physical or monetary donation for the collection of supplies for the development of simple disaster kits. A list of requested supplies is attached to this letter. As a result of your support, your business name and logo will be displayed prominently for the duration of the workshop, included in all printed materials, and verbally recognized to everyone present. If you are interested in making a donation, please select from the attached list the items you would like to donate, then purchase the items on https://www.walmart.com/lists/view-wish-list-items?id=5ad59f8b-e36a-4928-a6a3-f674eeddd041 website, the items will then be sent directly to me. If you would like to discuss my project further or send additional donations not listed above, please feel free to contact me directly by email. Thank you in advance for your assistance.

Sincerely,
The K.A.P.S. Team

Material for Implementing and Evaluating a K.A.P.S. Community Training

APPENDIX BOX C1 EXAMPLE: INFORMED CONSENT FORM

We invite you to participate in the K.A.P.S. Workshop conducted by the K.A.P.S. team. By consenting to participate, you acknowledge that you are a resident of <u>Geismar, Louisiana.</u> You also acknowledge that you will receive training on disasters and disaster preparedness. In participating in the workshop, you hereby agree to indemnify the entire K.A.P.S. training team, and all those (directly/indirectly) associated with the team against all damage, liability, claims, demands, expenses, actions, costs, and loss, as well as legal fees and costs incurred, as a result of participating in the workshop.

You will be given a questionnaire and asked to respond to 20 to 30 questions. The "before" questions focus on your existing knowledge of disaster preparedness, and the "after" questions are about what you learned during the workshop. You may skip any questions you want for any reason. The workshop will last approximately two hours and you can stop participating at any time. Potential benefits of your participation are an increased knowledge of how to prepare for disasters. The risks associated with your participation include reminders of past disasters; however, your participation is voluntary and at any time you can leave the workshop. You may discuss your participation with your family and friends.

You will be given a copy of this form. The information collected during the workshop will be included in an academic thesis tentatively entitled "Developing a Disaster Preparedness Tool Kit to Effectively Train the Community of Geismar, Louisiana in the Case of a Natural or Anthropogenic Disaster." To submit any other comments or concerns please feel free to contact the researcher by email at KAPSdisastertraining@gmail.com.

* * * * *

This form has been explained to me. I, _____, volunteer to take part in this workshop. I acknowledge that I have had a chance to ask questions. If I have questions later about the workshop, I can ask the workshop coordinator directly.

Signature	Date

APPENDIX BOX C2 EXAMPLE: RISK OF PARTICIPATION

Thank you for agreeing to take part in this workshop on disasters and disaster preparedness. The risk associated with taking part in this workshop includes but is not limited to reminders of past disasters and experiences. If discomfort arises at any time during the workshop, you may stop participating immediately. Your participation is voluntary and there will be no repercussions for leaving the workshop early. Your answers to any questionnaire will be discarded.

If discomfort does arise, please reach out to the Ascension Parish Counseling Agency by phone at 225-450-1016, or by visiting their office at East Ascension Complex Blvd, Gonzales, LA 70737. The Agency provides "comprehensive therapeutic services to individuals and families in an effort to foster healthy coping skills that will improve their quality of life." There is a small fee of $5.00 for all parish residents.

For any other comments or concerns please feel free to contact the workshop coordinator by email at KAPSdisastertraining@gmail.com.

APPENDIX BOX C3 EXAMPLE: PRE-SURVEY QUESTIONS

Instructions: This survey will be administered after the workshop to assess knowledge of disaster preparedness and your level of disaster readiness. Please fully complete the survey. The survey asks questions about your knowledge of disaster preparedness, as well as socioeconomic and demographic information.

Please answer YES or NO to the following questions:

1. Do you have nonperishable food readily available?
2. Do you have water readily available?
3. Do you have important paperwork like identification cards, insurance papers, bills, extra cash, credit cards, deeds/titles, health care information, etc. readily available?
4. Do you have an extra change of clothing readily available?
5. Do you have a list of emergency phone numbers readily available?
6. In the case of a natural or human-made disaster do you and your family have an evacuation plan?
7. Do you and your family have a disaster preparedness kit readily available?
8. Do you know where all the hospitals and emergency care facilities are in the case of a disaster?
9. Do you know which agencies to contact?
10. Do you know how to easily access Ascension Parish and/or Geismar's evacuation routes?
11. Do you know the location of the Ascension Parish/Geismar's emergency evacuation shelters?
12. Do you know what the local emergency radio and TV stations are and how to access those stations?
13. Do you know what it means to "Shelter in Place"?
14. Do you know the difference between a disaster warning and a disaster watch?
15. Have you ever attended a disaster preparedness workshop?
16. In the case of a hurricane can you decipher between the different hurricane categories and how to respond to each?
17. Do you know what to do when the community emergency alerting system sounds on days other than scheduled times?
18. In the case of a natural or human-made disaster do you know the fastest way to exit your house?
19. In the case of a natural or human-made disaster do you know the safest location in your house?
20. In the case of a natural or human-made disaster have you ever made any plans with a family member, friend, or neighbor to evacuate?

21. Do you know how to effectively respond in the case of a natural disaster or a human-made disaster?
22. Do you know the difference between a natural and human-made disaster?

On a scale of 1 to 5 please answer the following questions...

1. How responsive do you feel the local and national government organizations will be in addressing a natural or human-made disaster in your area?
2. How safe would a disaster preparedness plan make you feel?
3. How prepared are you in the case of a natural or human-made disaster?
4. How concerned are you about the possibility of a future human-made or natural disaster?
5. How concerned are you about losing your belongings as a result of a human-made and natural disaster?
6. How well do you know how to use the items in a disaster preparedness kit?

The following questions are regarding your socio demographic and socioeconomic background. Please mark the question that best describes your status.

1. Indicate your highest education level: _____
2. What is your current age? _____
3. What is your gender? _____
4. Do you own or rent your home? _____
5. Indicate your household income: _____
6. What is your race/ethnicity? _____

APPENDIX BOX C4 EXAMPLE: POST-SURVEY QUESTIONS

Instructions: This survey will be administered after the workshop to assess knowledge of disaster preparedness and your level of disaster readiness. Please fully complete the survey. The survey asks questions about your knowledge of disaster preparedness, as well as socioeconomic and demographic information.

Please answer YES or NO to the following questions:

As a result of the workshop ...

1. Will you prepare and ensure that nonperishable food and water is readily available in the event of a natural or human-made disaster?
2. Will you prepare and ensure that important paperwork like identification cards, insurance papers, bills; extra cash, credit cards, deeds, health care information, etc. are readily available in the event of a natural or human-made disaster?
3. Will you prepare and ensure that an extra change of clothing is readily available in the event of a natural or human-made disaster?
4. Do you now have a list of emergency phone numbers readily available in the case of a natural or human-made disaster?
5. Will you and your family develop an evacuation plan?
6. Will you and your family develop a disaster preparedness kit?
7. Do you now know where all the hospitals and emergency care facilities are in the case of a disaster?
8. Do you now know which agencies to contact in the case of a natural or human-made disaster?
9. Do you now know how to easily access Ascension Parish evacuation routes?
10. Do you now know the location of the Ascension Parish as well as Geismar's emergency evacuation shelters?
11. Do you now know how to access local radio stations and TV stations?
12. Do you now know what it means to properly "shelter in place"?
13. Do you now know the difference between a disaster warning and a disaster watch?
14. Have you ever attended a disaster preparedness workshop?
15. Do you know the difference between the hurricane categories and how to respond to each?
16. Do you now know what to do when the community emergency alerting system sounds on days other than scheduled times?
17. Do you now know the fastest way to exit your house in the case of a natural or human-made disaster?
18. Do you now know the safest place in your house in the case of a natural or human-made disaster?
19. Will you prepare plans with a family member, friend, or neighbor to evacuate in the case of a disaster?

20. Do you now know how to effectively respond in the case of a natural disaster or a human-made disaster?
21. Do you now know the difference between a natural and human-made disaster?

Please answer YES or NO to the following questions:

As a result of the workshop ...

1. Do you now know what it means to properly "shelter in place"?
2. Do you now know the difference between a disaster warning and a disaster watch?
3. Have you ever attended a disaster preparedness workshop?
4. Do you know the difference between the hurricane categories and how to respond to each?
5. Do you now know what to do when the community emergency alerting system sounds on days other than scheduled times?
6. Do you now know the fastest way to exit your house in the case of a natural or human-made disaster?
7. Do you now know the safest place in your house in the case of a natural or human-made disaster?
8. Will you prepare plans with a family member, friend, or neighbor to evacuate in the case of a disaster?
9. Do you now know how to effectively respond in the case of a natural disaster or a human-made disaster?
10. Do you now know the difference between a natural and human-made disaster?
11. Do you now know what it means to properly "shelter in place"?
12. Do you now know the difference between a disaster warning and a disaster watch?
13. Have you ever attended a disaster preparedness workshop?
14. Do you know the difference between the hurricane categories and how to respond to each?
15. Do you now know what to do when the community emergency alerting system sounds on days other than scheduled times?
16. Do you now know the fastest way to exit your house in the case of a natural or human-made disaster?
17. Do you now know the safest place in your house in the case of a natural or human-made disaster?
18. Will you prepare plans with a family member, friend, or neighbor to evacuate in the case of a disaster?
19. Do you now know how to effectively respond in the case of a natural disaster or a human-made disaster?
20. Do you now know the difference between a natural and human-made disaster?

On a scale of 1 to 5 please answer the following questions...

1. How safe would a disaster preparedness plan make you feel?
2. How likely are you to prepare a disaster preparedness plan?
3. How concerned are you about the possibility of a future human-made or natural disaster?
4. How concerned are you about losing your belongings as a result of a human-made and natural disaster?
5. How well do you know how to use the items in a disaster preparedness kit?

On a scale of 1 to 5 ...

1. Rate the workshop on effectiveness
2. Rate the workshop on clarity
3. Rate the workshop on interest
4. Rate the workshop on helpfulness
5. Rate the clarity of the information
6. Rate the quality of the presentation

The following questions are regarding your socio-demographic and socioeconomic background. Please mark the question that best describes your status.

1. Indicate your highest education level: _____
2. What is your current age? _____
3. What is your gender? _____
4. Do you own or rent your home? _____
5. Indicate your household income: _____
6. What is your race/ethnicity? _____

International and National Community Preparedness Resources

TABLE D1 International and National community resources.

Name of Resources	Agency	Type of Disaster	Country of Origin — National	International	Country	Source — Business	Non-profit	Individual	Household	Website
ADA Emergency Preparedness Resources	ADA	Natural/Pandemic	X		USA	X	X	X	X	https://adata.org/emergency-preparedness
All-Hazards Preparedness Guide	National Network	Human-made, Natural, Pandemic	X		USA	X	X	X	X	https://www.cdc.gov/cpr/documents/ahpg_final_march_2013.pdf
Be Informed	American Red Cross	Natural			USA	X	X		X	https://www.redcross.org/get-help/how-to-prepare-for-emergencies/be-informed.html
Best Practices in Protecting Your Home and Property from Hurricane Damage	American Red Cross	Natural	X		USA	X	X	X	X	https://preparednessguide.org/best-practices-in-protecting-your-home-property-from-hurricane-damage/
Chemical Emergency Preparedness	American Red Cross: Preparedness Guide	Human-made			USA	X	X	X	X	https://www.redcross.org/get-help/how-to-prepare-for-emergencies/types-of-emergencies/chemical-emergency.html

(Continued)

Table D1 (Continued)

Name of Resources	Agency	Type of Disaster	National	International	Country	Business	Non-profit	Individual	Household	Website
Comprehensive Preparedness Guides	FEMA	Natural	x		USA	x	x	x	x	https://www.fema.gov/emergency-managers/national-preparedness/plan
Coronavirus Safety	American Red Cross	Pandemic			USA	x	x	x	x	https://www.redcross.org/get-help/how-to-prepare-for-emergencies/types-of-emergencies/coronavirus-safety.html
Disaster Preparedness	European Civil Protection and Humanitarian and Operations	Natural, Human-made,		x		x	x			https://ec.europa.eu/echo/what/humanitarian-aid/disaster_preparedness_en
Disaster Relief & Recovery	Conrad N. Hilton Foundation	Natural/Human-made			USA	x	x		x	https://www.hiltonfoundation.org/priorities/disaster-relief-and-recovery
Emergency Preparedness Tips	Nationwide	Natural			USA	x	x			https://www.nationwide.com/lc/resources/emergency-preparedness/articles/catastrophe-preparation
Emergency Preparedness, Response and Recovery Guide	International Chamber of Commerce	Natural		x		x	x			https://iccwbo.org/publication/emergency-preparedness-response-recovery-guide/

Resource	Organization	Type		Country				URL
Emergency Response Preparedness	Inter-Agency Standing Committee	Natural		USA	x	x		https://interagencystandingcommittee.org/system/files/iasc_emergency_response_preparedness_guidelines_july_2015_draft_for_field_testing.pdf
FEMA Preparedness Grants Manual	FEMA	Natural	x	USA	x	x	x	https://www.fema.gov/grants/preparedness/manual
Get a Game Plan Louisiana Grants	Get a Game Plan	Natural	x	USA	x	x	x	https://www.getagameplan.org/
Grants.gov	Grants.gov	Natural		USA	X	X		http://www.grants.gov/
Hurricanes, Severe Storms, and COVID-19	CDC	Natural	x	USA	x	x	x	https://www.cdc.gov/disasters/hurricanes/covid-19/prepare-for-hurricane.html
International Network: Emergency Preparedness and Response (EPR)	IAEA	Natural		USA	x	x	x	https://www.iaea.org/topics/international-framework
Local Area Preparedness Guides	The Church of Latter Day Saints	Human-made, Natural, Pandemic		USA	x	x	x	https://www.churchofjesuschrist.org/life/AreaPreparednessGuides?lang=eng

(Continued)

Table D1 (Continued)

Name of Resources	Agency	Type of Disaster	Country of Origin			Source				Website
			National	International	Country	Business	Non-profit	Individual	Household	
Louisiana Governor's Office of Elderly Affairs	CDC	Natural			USA			x	x	http://goea.louisiana.gov/index.cfm?md=pagebuilder&tmp=home&pid=13&pnid=0&nid=10
Louisiana Emergency Preparedness Guides	Office of Homeland Security and Emergency Preparedness	Natural			USA	x	x	x		http://gohsep.la.gov/PREPARE/EMERGENCY-PREPAREDNESS-GUIDE
National Hurricane Preparedness Month	National Weather Service	Natural			USA	x	x			https://www.weather.gov/wrn/hurricane-preparedness
Novel Coronavirus (2019-nCoV): Strategic Preparedness and Response Plan	WHO	Human-made, Natural, Pandemic			USA	x	x	x	x	https://www.who.int/publications-detail-redirect/strategic-preparedness-and-response-plan-for-the-new-coronavirus
PA Emergency Preparedness Guide	American Red Cross	Human-made, Natural, Pandemic	x		USA	x	x	x	x	https://www.ready.pa.gov/BeInformed/EmergencyPreparednessGuide/Pages/default.aspx
Preparedness	Florida Division of Emergency Management	Natural	x		USA	x	x			https://www.floridadisaster.org/dem/preparedness/

Name	Organization	Hazard		Country					URL
Preparedness	Hagerty Emergency Management Consulting Firm	Natural	X	USA	X				https://hagertyconsulting.com/our-work/preparedness/
Preparedness: Are You Ready?	Houston Office Emergency Preparedness	Natural	X	USA	X	X	X	X	https://www.houstonoem.org/preparedness-are-you-ready/
Preparedness for Older Adults – A Guide for Those Who Live with or Love Senior Citizens	The National Academies Press	Natural	X	USA	X	X	X	X	https://preparednessguide.org/preparedness-for-older-adults-a-guide-for-those-who-live-with-or-love-senior-citizens/
Ready Pandemic	FEMA	Pandemic		USA	X	X			https://www.ready.gov/pandemic
Ready California	California Governor's Office of Emergency Services	Natural		USA	X	X			https://www.caloes.ca.gov/ICESite/Pages/National-Preparedness-Month.aspx
Ready New York	NYEM	Natural		USA	X	X			https://www1.nyc.gov/site/em/ready/ready-new-york.page
Ready.gov	FEMA	Natural	X	USA	X	X	X		https://www.ready.gov/
Ready.gov/ business	FEMA	Natural	X	USA	X	X	X		https://www.ready.gov/business

(Continued)

Table D1 (Continued)

Name of Resources	Agency	Type of Disaster	Country of Origin			Source				Website
			National	International	Country	Business	Non-profit	Individual	Household	
Red Cross Canada	Red Cross		X		Canada					https://www.redcross.ca/blog/category/emergency-preparedness
Reference Materials: Preparedness Links	International Association of Emergency Managers	Natural		X		X	X			https://www.iaem.org/resources/reference-materials/preparedness
Small Steps Toward Being Prepared for an Emergency	Do 1 Thing Emergency Preparedness	Natural	X		USA	X	X			http://do1thing.com/
Training + Certification: Simple, Fast, And Easy	American Red Cross	Natural			USA	X	X	X		https://www.redcross.org/take-a-class
Types of Emergencies and How to Prepare	American Red Cross	Human-made, Natural, Pandemic			USA	X	X	X		https://www.redcross.org/get-help/how-to-prepare-for-emergencies/types-of-emergencies.html

Bibliography

Abarquez, I., and Murshed, Z. (2004). Field Practitioners' Handbook. Bangkok: Asian Disaster Preparedness Center.

Adger, W. N., and Brooks, N. (2003). Does global environmental change cause vulnerability to disaster? In M. Pelling (ed.) Natural Disaster and Development in a Globalising World. London: Routledge, pp. 35–58.

Adger, W. N., and Vincent, K. (2005). Uncertainty in adaptive capacity. *Comptes Rendus Geoscience*, 337(4), 399–410.

Albanese, M. A., and Mitchell, S. (1993). Problem-based learning: a review of the literature on its outcomes and implementation issues. *Academic Medicine*, 68(1), 52–81.

Allmendinger, P. (2009). Planning Theory (2nd ed.). New York: Palgrave Macmillan.

Aldrich, D. P., and Meyer, M. A. (2015). Social capital and community resilience. *American Behavioral Scientist*, 59(2), 254–269.

Alvarez, K., Salas, E., and Garofano, C. M. (2004). An integrated model of training evaluation and effectiveness. *Human Resource Development Review*, 3(4), 385–416.

American Public Health Association (APHA) (2019). Addressing Environmental Justice to Achieve Health Equity. Policy No. 20197. Online. Available HTTP: https://www.apha.org/policies-and-advocacy/public-health-policy-statements/policy-database/2020/01/14/addressing-environmental-justice-to-achieve-health-equity. Accessed 9 January, 2022.

Anderson, W. A. (1965). Some observations on a disaster subculture: the organizational response of Cincinnati, Ohio, to the 1964 flood. Disaster Research Center: *Research Notes*, 6.

Anguiano, C., Milstein, T., De Larkin, I., Chen, Y. W., and Sandoval, J. (2012). Connecting community voices: using a Latino/a critical race theory lens on environmental justice advocacy. *Journal of International and Intercultural Communication*, 5(2), 124–143.

Arends, R. I. (1998). Resource Handbook. Learning to Teach (4th ed.). Boston, MA: McGraw-Hill.

Armstrong, P. (2016). Bloom's taxonomy. Vanderbilt University Center for Teaching. Online. Available HTTP: https://cft.vanderbilt.edu/guides-sub-pages/blooms-taxonomy/. Accessed: 22 December, 2021.

Arroyo, C. G., and Zigler, E. (1995). Racial identity, academic achievement, and the psychological well-being of economically disadvantaged adolescents. *Journal of Personality and Social Psychology, 69*, 903–914.

Asthma and Allergy Foundation of America. (2021). Climate and Health. Online. Available HTTP: https://www.aafa.org/climate-and-health/. Accessed: 22 December, 2021.

Babajanian, B. (2009). Decentralised Governance and Poverty Reduction in Kyrgyzstan. London: London School of Economics.

Babbie, E. R. (2013). The Practice of Social Research (13th ed.). Belmont, CA: Wadsworth Cengage Learning.

Babbie, E., and Mouton, J. (2001). The Practice of Social Science Research. Belmont, CA: Wadsworth.

Bahadur, A., Lovell, E., and Pichon, F. (2016). Effectiveness in building resilience: Synthesis report for Oxfam's Resilience Outcome Area, Oxfam. Online. Available HTTP: https://oxfamilibrary.openrepository.com/bitstream/handle/10546/620103/er-effectiveness-resilience-building-080216-en.pdf?sequence=1&isAllowed=y. Accessed: 22 December 2021.

Banks, L. (2013). Caring for elderly adults during disasters. *Southern Medical Journal* 106(1): 94–98.

Barnes, M., and Schmitz, P. (2016). Community engagement matters (now more than ever). *Stanford Social Innovation Review*, 14(2), 32–39.

Bartomeus, I., Potts, S. G., Steffan-Dewenter, I., Vaissière, B. E., Woyciechowski, M., Krewenka, K. M., Tscheulin, T., Roberts, S. P., Szentgyörgyi, H., Westphal, C., and Bommarco, R. (2014). Contribution of insect pollinators to crop yield and quality varies with agricultural intensification. *PeerJ*, 2, e328. 10.7717/peerj.328

Basolo, V., Steinberg, L. J., Burby, R. J., Levine, J., Cruz, A. M., and Huang, C. (2009). The effects of confidence in government and information on perceived and actual preparedness for disasters. *Environment and Behavior*, 41(3), 338–364.

Bassier, A., Fogle, N., and Taverno, R. (2008). Developing Effective Citizen Engagement: A How-To Guide for Community Leaders. Harrisberg: The Center for Rural Pennsylvania.

Baudoin, M. A., Henly-Shepard, S., Fernando, N., Sitati, A., and Zommers, Z. (2016). From top-down to "community-centric" approaches to early warning systems: exploring pathways to improve disaster risk reduction through community participation. *International Journal of Disaster Risk Science*, 7(2), 163–174.

Beaulieu, L. J. (2014). Promoting Community Vitality and Sustainability: The Community Capitals Framework. Purdue University, 1–7. Online. Available HTTP: https://pcrd.purdue.edu/wp-content/uploads/2020/09/Community-Capitals-Framework-Writeup-Oct-2014.pdf. Accessed: 22 December 2021.

Becker, J. S., Paton, D., Johnston, D. M., and Ronan, K. R. (2012). A model of household preparedness for earthquakes: how individuals make meaning of earthquake information and how this influences preparedness. *Natural Hazards*, 64(1), 107–137.

Berke, P., Cooper, J., Salvesen, D., Spurlock, D., and Rausch, C. (2011). Building capacity for disaster resiliency in six disadvantaged communities. *Sustainability*, 3(1), 1–20.

Berkes, F., Colding, J., and Folke, C. (2000). Rediscovery of traditional ecological knowledge as adaptive management. *Ecological Applications*, 10(5), 1251–1262.

Bethel, J. W., Burke, S. C., and Britt, A. F. (2013). Disparity in disaster preparedness between racial/ethnic groups. *Disaster Health*, 1(2), 110–116.

Blaikie, P., Cannon, T., Davis, I., and Wisner, B. (1994). At Risk: Natural Hazards, People's Vulnerability and Disasters. London: Routledge.

Blanks, J., Abuabara, A., Roberts, A., and Semien, J. (2021). Preservation at the intersections: patterns of disproportionate multi-hazard risk and vulnerability in Louisiana's historic African American cemeteries. *Environmental Justice*, 14(1), 1–13.

Blom-Hoffman, J., Wilcox, K. R., Dunn, L., Leff, S. S., and Power, T. J. (2008). Family involvement in school-based health promotion: bringing nutrition information home. *School Psychology Review*, 37(4), 567–577.

Bloom, B. S. with Englehart, M. D., Furst, E. J., Hill, W. H. and Krathwohl, D. R. (1956). Taxonomy of Educational Objectives, Handbook 1: Cognitive Domain. London: Longmans.

Bolin, B., and Kurtz, L. C. (2017). Race, class, ethnicity, and disaster vulnerability. In H. Rodriguez, J. Trainor, and W. Donner (eds) Handbook of Disaster Research (2nd ed.). New York: Springer, pp. 181–204.

Bolin, R. C., and Bolton, P. A. (1986). Race, Religion, and Ethnicity in Disaster Recovery. Institute of Behavioral Science, University of Colorado.

Bolin, R., Jackson, M., and Crist, A. (1998). Gender inequality, vulnerability, and disaster: Issues in theory and research. In E. Enarson and B. H. Morrow (eds) The Gendered Terrain of Disaster: Through Women's Eyes, Westport: Praeger, pp. 27–44.

Bos, D. G., and Brown, H. L. (2015). Overcoming barriers to community participation in a catchment-scale experiment: building trust and changing behavior. *Freshwater Science*, 34(3), 1169–1175.

Bourque, L. B., Regan, R., Kelley, M. M., Wood, M. M., Kano, M., and Mileti, D. S. (2013). An examination of the effect of perceived risk on preparedness behavior. *Environment and Behavior*, 45(5), 615–649.

Bowen, T., and Marks, J. (1994). Inside Teaching. Oxford: Heinemann English Language Teaching.

Brailas, A., Koskinas, K., and Alexias, G. (2017). Teaching to emerge: toward a bottom-up pedagogy. *Cogent Education*, 4(1), 1377506.

Brett, J., and Oviatt, K. (2013). The intrinsic link of vulnerability to sustainable development. In D. S. K. Thomas, B. D. Phillips, W. E. Lovekamp and A. Fothergill (eds) Social Vulnerability to Disasters (2nd ed.). Boca Raton, Fl: CRC Press, pp. 57–82.

Bronfenbrenner, U. (1974). Developmental research, public policy, and the ecology of childhood. *Child Development*, 45(1), 1–5.

Bronfenbrenner, U. (1977). Toward an experimental ecology of human development. *American Psychologist*, 32(7), 513.

Bronfenbrenner, U. (1995). Developmental ecology through space and time: a future perspective. In P. Moen, G. H. Elder Jr., and K. Lüscher (eds), Examining Lives in Context: Perspectives on the Ecology of Human Development. Washington, DC: American Psychological Association, pp. 619–647.

Bronfenbrenner, U., and Evans, G. W. (2000). Developmental science in the 21st century: emerging questions, theoretical models, research designs and empirical findings. *Social Development*, 9(1), 115–125.

Bronfenbrenner, U., and Morris, P. A. (1998). The ecology of developmental processes. In W. Damon and R. M. Lerner (eds), Handbook of Child Psychology, Vol. 1: Theoretical Models of Human Development (5th ed.). New York: Wiley, pp. 993–1023.

Brooks, M. P. (2002). Planning Theory for Practitioners. Chicago, IL: Planners Press, American Planning Association.

Brown, K. G., and Gerhardt, M. W. (2002). Formative evaluation: an integrative practice model and case study. *Personnel Psychology*, 55(4), 951–983.

Bullard, R. D. (2007). Equity, unnatural man-made disasters, and race: why environmental justice matters. *Equity and the Environment*, 15, 1–18.

Bullard, R. D. (2008). Differential vulnerabilities: environmental and economic inequality and government response to unnatural disasters. *Social Research*, 753–784.

Bullard, R. D., and Johnson, G. S. (2000). Environmentalism and public policy: environmental justice: grassroots activism and its impact on public policy decision making. *Journal of Social Issues*, 56(3), 555–578.

Bullard, R. D., and Wright, B. (2008). Disastrous response to natural and man-made disasters: an environmental justice analysis twenty-five years after Warren County. *UCLA Journal of Environmental Law and Policy*, 26, 217.

Bullard, R. D., and Wright, B. (2009). Race, Place, and Environmental Justice After Hurricane Katrina: Struggles to Reclaim, Rebuild, and Revitalize New Orleans and the Gulf Coast. New York: Perseus Books.

Bullard, R. D., Johnson, G. S., and Torres, A. O. (2009). African Americans on the front line of environmental assault. *Health Issues in the Black Community*, 3, 177–208.

Bullard, R. D., Johnson, G. S., King, D. W., and Smith, S. L. (2014). People of color on the frontline of environmental assault. In J. Hall (ed.) Underprivileged School Children and the Assault on Dignity. London: Routledge, pp. 19–47.

Bullard, R. D., Mohaj, P., Saha, R., and Wright, B. (2008). Toxic wastes and race at twenty: why race still matters after all of these years. *Environmental Law* 38(2), 371–411.

Burnside, R., Miller, D. S., and Rivera, J. D. (2007). The impact of information and risk perception on the hurricane evacuation decision-making of greater New Orleans residents. *Sociological Spectrum*, 27(6), 727–740.

Burton H., Adams M., Bunton R., and Schroder-Back P. (2008). Developing stakeholder involvement for introducing public health genomics into public policy. *Public Health Genomics*, 12, 11–19.

Butler, C., and Adamowski, J. (2015). Empowering marginalized communities in water resources management: addressing inequitable practices in participatory model building. *Journal of Environmental Management*, 153, 153–162.

Cafaro, P. (2015). Three ways to think about the sixth mass extinction. *Biological Conservation*, 192, 387–393.

Campbell, H., and Marshall, R. (2002). Utilitarianism's bad breath? A re-evaluation of the public interest justification for planning. *Planning Theory*, 1(2), 163–187.

Cannon, T. (2015). Disasters, climate change and the significance of 'culture'. In F. Krüger, G. Bankoff, T. Cannon, B. Orlowski, E. L. F. Schipper (eds) Cultures and Disasters: Understanding Cultural Framings in Disaster Risk Reduction. London: Routledge, pp. 88–106.

Carrington, D. (2014). Earth has lost half of its wildlife in the past 40 years, says WWF. *The Guardian*. Online. Available HTTP: https://www.theguardian.com/environment/2014/sep/29/earth-lost-50-wildlife-in-40-years-wwf. Accessed 22 December, 2021.

Carson, E. A. (2020). Prisoners in 2018. US Department of Justice: Bureau of Justice Statistics. Online. Available HTTP: https://bjs.ojp.gov/content/pub/pdf/p18.pdf. Accessed 22 December, 2021.

Casey, J. (2011). Understanding advocacy: A primer on the policy-making role of nonprofit organizations. New York: Baruch College, City University of New York, Center for Nonprofit Strategy. Online. Available HTTP: https://marxe.baruch.cuny.edu/wp-content/uploads/sites/7/2020/04/Casey_UnderstandingAdvocacyaPrimeronthePolicyMaking RoleofNonprofitOrganizations.pdf. Accessed 22 December, 2021.

Ceballos, G., Ehrlich, P. R., and Dirzo, R. (2017). "Biological annihilation via the ongoing sixth mass extinction signaled by vertebrate population losses and declines". Proceedings of the National Academy of Science. 114 (30), E6089–E6096.

Chakraborty, J., Collins, T. W., and Grineski, S. E. (2019). Exploring the environmental justice implications of Hurricane Harvey flooding in Greater Houston, Texas. *American Journal of Public Health*, 109, 244–250.

Chamlee-Wright, E., and Storr, V. H. (2011). Social capital as collective narratives and post-disaster community recovery. *The Sociological Review*, 59(2), 266–282.

Chandrasekhar, D. (2012). Digging deeper: participation and non-participation in post-disaster community recovery. *Community Development*, 43(5), 614–629.

Chikoto, G. L., Sadiq, A. A., and Fordyce, E. (2013). Disaster mitigation and preparedness: comparison of nonprofit, public, and private organizations. *Nonprofit and Voluntary Sector Quarterly*, 42(2), 391–410.

Chikoto-Schultz, G. L., Russo, A., Manson, P., and White, J. (2018). Oregon nonprofit disaster preparedness: finding from the 2018 survey. The Nonprofit Institute Research. 2. Online. Available HTTP: https://archives.pdx.edu/ds/psu/27233. Accessed 22 December, 2021.

Christopher, S., Watts, V., McCormick, A. K. H. G., and Young, S. (2008). Building and maintaining trust in a community-based participatory research partnership. *American Journal of Public Health*, 98(8), 1398–1406.

Coastal Protection Restoration Authority. (2017). Coastal Master Plan: Baton Rouge, Louisiana, pp. 1–93.

Coffey, J., Huff-Davis, A., Lindsey, C., Norman, O., Curtis, H., Criner, C., and Stewart, M. K. (2017). The development of a community engagement workshop: a community-led approach for building researcher capacity. *Progress in Community Health Partnerships: Research, Education, and Action*, 11(3), 321–329.

Colding, J., and Folke, C. (2001). Social taboos: "invisible" systems of local resource management and biological conservation. *Ecological Applications*, 11(2), 584–600.

Comfort, L. K., Thomas A. B., Beverly, A. C., and Nance, E. (2010). Retrospectives and prospectives on Hurricane Katrina – five years and counting, *Public Administration Review*, 70(5), 669–678.

Congressional Black Caucus Foundation, Inc. (2004). African Americans and Climate Change: An Unequal Burden. Online. Available HTTP: https://23u0pr24qn4zn4d4qinlmyh8-wpengine.netdna-ssl.com/wp-content/uploads/2013/02/CBCF_REPORT_F.pdf. Accessed 24 December, 2021.

Connolly, M. (2012). Creating a campus-based community emergency response team (CERT). *Community College Journal of Research and Practice*, 36(6), 448–452.

Corburn, J. (2003). Bringing local knowledge into environmental decision making: Improving urban planning for communities at risk. *Journal of Planning Education and Research*, 22(4), 420–433.

Crawford, B. F., Snyder, K. E., and Adelson, J. L. (2020). Exploring obstacles faced by gifted minority students through Bronfenbrenner's bioecological systems theory. *High Ability Studies*, 31(1), 43–74.

Crawford, P., Kotval, Z., Rauhe, W., and Kotval-K, Z. (2008). Social capital development in participatory community planning and design. *The Town Planning Review*, 533–553.

Cutter, S. L., Boruff, B. J., and Shirley, W. L. (2003). Social vulnerability to environmental hazards. *Social Science Quarterly*, 84(2), 242–261.

Cutter, S. L., Barnes, L., Berry, M., Burton, C., Evans, E., Tate, E., and Webb, J. (2008). A place-based model for understanding community resilience to natural disasters. *Global Environmental Change*, 18(4), 598–606.

Dash, N. (2013). Race and ethnicity. In D. S. K. Thomas, B. D. Phillips, W. E. Lovekamp and A. Fothergill (eds) Social Vulnerability to Disasters (2nd ed.). Boca Raton, Fl: CRC Press, pp. 113–138.

Davidoff, P. (1965). Advocacy and pluralism in planning. *Journal of the American Institute of Planners*, 31(4), 270–338.

Davis, E. A., Hansen, R., Kett, M., Mincin, J., and Twigg, J. (2013). Disability. In D. S. K. Thomas, B. D. Phillips, W. E. Lovekamp and A. Fothergill (eds) Social Vulnerability to Disasters (2nd ed.). Boca Raton, Fl: CRC Press, p. 199.

De Graaf, E., and Kolmos, A. (2003). Characteristics of problem-based learning. *International Journal of Engineering Education*, 19(5), 657–662.

De Winter, J. C., and Dodou, D. (2010). Five-point Likert items: t test versus Mann-Whitney-Wilcoxon. *Practical Assessment, Research and Evaluation*, 15(11), 1–16.

Dewey, J. (1986) Experience and education. *The Educational Forum*, 50(3), 241–252.

Dekens, J. (2007). Local knowledge for disaster preparedness: A literature review. International Centre for Integrated Mountain Development (ICIMOD). Available HTTP: https://lib.icimod.org/record/22470 Accessed 24 December, 2021.

Department of Homeland Security (DHS). (2021). Natural disasters. Online. Available HTTP: https://www.dhs.gov/natural-disasters. Accessed 24 December, 2021.

Despart, Z., and Scherer, J. (2021). Houston and Harris County asked for $1.3B in flood aid. The GLO's offer: $0. *Houston Chronicle*. Online. Available https://www.houstonchronicle.com/news/houston-texas/houston/article/Houston-and-Harris-County-asked-for-1-3B-in-16192647.php Accessed 24 December, 2021.

Dreier, Hannah. (2021). FEMA pressed on historically high rejection rates for disaster survivors. *The Washington Post*, 23 June. Online. Available https://www.washingtonpost.com/national/fema-pressed-on-historically-high-rejection-rates-for-disaster-survivors/2021/06/23/40edf97c-d43a-11eb-ae54-515e2f63d37d_story.html Accessed 24 December, 2021.

Dreier, H. and Tran, A. B. (2021). The real damage: why FEMA is denying disaster aid to Black families that have lived for generations in the Deep South. *The Washington Post*, 11 June. Online. Available HTTP: https://www.washingtonpost.com/nation/2021/07/11/fema-black-owned-property/ Accessed 24 December, 2021.

Duch, B. J., Groh, S. E., and Allen, D. E. (2001). The Power of Problem-Based Learning: A Practical "How To" For Teaching Undergraduate Courses in Any Discipline. Sterling, VA: Stylus Publishing, LLC.

Eade, D. (2007). Capacity building: who builds whose capacity? *Development in Practice*, 17(4–5), 630–639.

Eagly, A. H., and Chaiken, S. (1993). The Psychology of Attitudes. New York: Harcourt Brace Jovanovich College Publishers.

Eisenman, D. P., Cordasco, K. M., Asch, S., Golden, J. F., and Glik, D. (2007). Disaster planning and risk communication with vulnerable communities: lessons from Hurricane Katrina. *American Journal of Public Health*, 97 (Supplement_1), S109–S115.

Eliasson, I. (2000). The use of climate knowledge in urban planning. *Landscape and Urban Planning*, 48(1–2), 31–44.

Elliott, A. (2021). Contemporary Social Theory: An Introduction. London: Routledge.

Elliott, J., Loughran, K., and Brown, P. L. (2021). Divergent Residential Pathways from Flood-Prone Areas: How Neighborhood Inequalities Are Shaping Urban Climate Adaptation. Online. Available HTTP: https://hdl.handle.net/1911/110847. Accessed 24 December, 2021.

Elliott, S. N., Kratochwill, T. R., Littlefield Cook, J. and Travers, J. (2000). Educational Psychology: Effective Teaching, Effective Learning (3rd ed.). Boston, MA: McGraw-Hill College.

Elsasser, S. W., and Dunlap, R. E. (2013). Leading voices in the denier choir: conservative columnists' dismissal of global warming and denigration of climate science. *American Behavioral Scientist*, 57(6) 754–776.

Enarson, E., and Fordham, M. (2000). Lines that divide, ties that bind: race, class, and gender in women's flood recovery in the US and UK. *Australian Journal of Emergency Management*, 15(4), 43–52.

Enarson, E., Fothergill, A., and Peek, L. (2018). Gender and disaster: foundations and new directions for research and practice. In H. Rodríguez, W. Donner, and J. E. Trainor (eds) Handbook of Disaster Research. New York: Springer, pp. 205–223.

Enenkel, M., Papp, A., Veit, E., and Voigt, S. (2017). Top-down and bottom-up—a global approach to strengthen local disaster resilience. 2017 IEEE Global Humanitarian Technology Conference (GHTC). IEEE, pp. 1–7.

Environmental Protection Agency (EPA). (n.d.). Community Profiles. Community Involvement Tool. Online. Available HTTP: https://semspub.epa.gov/work/HQ/100001429.pdf. Accessed 24 December, 2021.

Environmental Protection Agency (EPA). (n.d.). Superfund Community Involvement Tools and Resources. Online. Available HTTP: https://www.epa.gov/superfund/superfund-community-involvement-tools-and-resources#files. Accessed 24 December, 2021.

Fainstein, S. S., and DeFilippis, J. (2015). Readings in Planning Theory. Oxford: John Wiley and Sons.

Faupel, C. E., Kelley, S. P. and Petee, T. (1992). The impact of disaster education on household preparedness for Hurricane Hugo. *International Journal of Mass Emergencies and Disasters* 10(1), 5–24.

Fernandez, G., and Ahmed, I. (2019). 'Build back better' approach to disaster recovery: Research trends since 2006. *Progress in Disaster Science*, 1, 100003.

Fernando, S. Y., and Marikar, F. M. (2017). Constructivist teaching/learning theory and participatory teaching methods. *Journal of Curriculum and Teaching*, 6(1), 110–122.

Fieser, J. (2009). Great issues in philosophy. Online. Available HTTP: www.utm. edu/staff/jfieser/120. Accessed 24 December, 2021.

Finch, C., Emrich, C. T., and Cutter, S. L. (2010). Disaster disparities and differential recovery in New Orleans. *Population and Environment*, 31(4), 179–202.

Finucane, P. M., Johnson, S. M., and Prideaux, D. J. (1998). Problem-based learning: its rationale and efficacy. *Medical Journal of Australia*, 168(9), 445–448.

Fleming, N. D., and Mills, C. (1992). Not another inventory, rather a catalyst for reflection. *To Improve the Academy*, 11, 137–155.

Flint, C., and Brennan, M. (2006). Community emergency response teams: from disaster responders to community builders. *Rural Realities*, 1(3), 1–9.

Fordham, M., Lovekamp, W. E., Thomas, D. S. K., and Phillips, B. D. (2013). Understanding social vulnerability. In D. S. K. Thomas, B. D. Phillips, W. E. Lovekamp and A. Fothergill (eds) Social Vulnerability to Disasters (2nd ed.). Boca Raton, Fl: CRC Press, p. 1–32.

Fothergill, A., and Peek, L. A. (2004). Poverty and disasters in the United States: a review of recent sociological findings. *Natural Hazards*, 32(1), 89–110.

Fothergill, A., Maestas, E. G., and Darlington, J. D. (1999). Race, ethnicity and disasters in the United States: A review of the literature. *Disasters*, 23(2), 156–173.

Frank, T. (2021). Billion-dollar disasters shattered U.S. record in 2020. *Scientific American*, 11 January, 2021. Online. Available HTTP: https://www.scientificamerican.com/article/billion-dollar-disasters-shattered-u-s-record-in-2020/.

Frankenberg, E., Sikoki, B., Sumantri, C., Suriastini, W., and Thomas, D. (2013). Education, vulnerability, and resilience after a natural disaster. *Ecology and Society: A Journal of Integrative Science for Resilience and Sustainability*, 18(2), 16.

Freire, P. (1996). *Pedagogy of the Oppressed* (revised). New York: Continuum.

Gaillard, J. C., and Mercer, J. (2013). From knowledge to action: bridging gaps in disaster risk reduction. *Progress in Human Geography*, 37(1), 93–114.

Garbero, A., and Muttarak, R. (2013). Impacts of the 2010 droughts and floods on community welfare in rural Thailand: differential effects of village educational attainment. *Ecology and Society*, 18(4), 1–18.

García, J. M. R. (2001). Scientia Potestas Est–Knowledge is Power: Francis Bacon to Michel Foucault. *Neohelicon*, 28(1), 109–121.

Gibson, M. J., and Hayunga, M. (2006). We Can Do Better: Lessons Learned for Protecting Older Persons in Disasters. Washington, DC: AA GraphPad Statistics Guide.

Gilmore, R. W. (2002). Fatal couplings of power and difference: Notes on racism and geography. *The Professional Geographer*, 54(1), 15–24.

Glantz, M. H. (2012). Africans, African-Americans and climate impacts: top down vs. bottom-up approach to capacity building. In G. Johnson, S. A. Rainey-Brown, and R. D. S. Gragg. Environmental Justice Reader, II. Ronkonkoma, N.Y.: Linus Publications, pp. 423–425.

Gleick, P. (2019). Atmospheric CO_2 levels have now reached 415 ppm. Twitter update. Online. Available HTTP: https://twitter.com/PeterGleick/status/1127960911094865920. Accessed 24 December, 2021.

Goodall, C. (2015). Working with difficult to reach groups: a 'building blocks' approach to researching trust in communities. In F. Lyon, G. Mšllering, and M. N. Saunders (eds). Handbook of Research Methods on Trust. Cheltenham: Edward Elgar Publishing.

Gormally, S. (2012). A social justice approach to community development. *The Irish Journal of Community Work*, 1(3), 16–28.

Gregorio, J. D., and Lee, J. W. (2002). Education and income inequality: new evidence from cross-country data. *Review of Income and Wealth*, 48(3), 395–416.

Gruber, N., Clement, D., Carter, B. R., Feely, R. A., Van Heuven, S., Hoppema, M., Ishii, M., Key, R. M., Kozyr, A., Lauvset, S. K., et al. (2019). The oceanic sink for anthropogenic CO_2 from 1994 to 2007. *Science*, 15 Mar 2019: 363 (6432), pp. 1193–1199.

Gundlach, M. and McDonough, M. (2011). Top-down vs. bottom-up planning. Online. Available HTTP: http://www.brighthubpm.com/project-planning/8542-top-down-vs-bottom-up-planning/. Accessed 10 January 2021.

Guy, S. (2006). Designing urban knowledge: competing perspectives on energy and buildings. *Environment and Planning C: Government and Policy*, 24(5), 645–659.

Hambrick, K. (2021). Personal interview, 15 June.

Hanssen, G. S. (2010). Ensuring local community interests in market-oriented urban planning? The role of local politicians. *Environment and Planning C: Government and Policy*, 28(4), 714–732.

Harden, M. (2021). Personal interview, 15 August.

Harlan, S. L., Pellow, D. N. and Roberts J. T. withBell, S. E., Holt, W. G., and Nagel J. (2015) Climate injustice and inequality: insights from sociology. In R. E. Dunlap and R. J. Brulle (eds) Climate Change and Society: Sociological Perspectives. Oxford: Oxford University Press, pp. 127–163.

Haynes, G. W., Danes, S. M., Schrank, H. L., and Lee, Y. (2019). Survival and success of family-owned small businesses after Hurricane Katrina: impact of disaster assistance and adaptive capacity. *Journal of Contingencies and Crisis Management*, 27(2), 130–144.

Haynes, K., Coates, L., Leigh, R., Handmer, J., Whittaker, J., Gissing, A., McAneney, J. and Opper, S. (2009). "Shelter-in-place" vs. evacuation in flash floods. *Environmental Hazards*, 8(4), 291–303.

Helne, T. and Salonen, A. O. (2016) Ecosocial food policy: improving human, animal, and planetary well-being, *Sustainability: Science, Practice and Policy*, 12(2), 1–11.

Hemmerling, S. A., Barra, M., Bienn, H. C., Baustian, M. M., Jung, H., Meselhe, E., Wang, Y., and White, E. (2020). Elevating local knowledge through participatory modeling: active community engagement in restoration planning in coastal Louisiana. *Journal of Geographical Systems*, 22(2), 241–266.

Hernandez, P. (2021). Personal interview, 15 May.

Hewitt, K. (1983). Place annihilation: area bombing and the fate of urban places. *Annals of the Association of American Geographers*, 73(2), 257–284.

Highfield, W. E., Peacock, W. G., and Van Zandt, S. (2014). Mitigation planning: why hazard exposure, structural vulnerability, and social vulnerability matter. *Journal of Planning Education and Research*, 34(3), 287–300.

Hino, M. and Nance, E. (2021). Five ways to ensure flood-risk research helps the most vulnerable. *Nature*, 595, 27–29.

Hoffmann, R., and Muttarak, R. (2017). Learn from the past, prepare for the future: impacts of education and experience on disaster preparedness in the Philippines and Thailand. *World Development*, 96, 32–51.

Hofrichter, R. (1993). Cultural activism and environmental justice. In R. Hofrichter (ed.) Toxic Struggles: The Theory and Practice of Environmental Justice. Philadelphia, PA: New Society, pp. 85–97.

Hogg, M., and Vaughan, G. (2005). Social Psychology (4th ed.). London: Prentice-Hall.

Holthaus, E. (2019). This is the first time in human history our planet's atmosphere has had more than 415ppm CO_2. Twitter update, 12 May. Online. Available HTTP: https://twitter. com/EricHolthaus/status/1127681719216353280. Accessed 24 December, 2021.

Horton, M., and Freire, P. (1990). We Make the Road by Walking: Conversations on Education and Social Change. Pennsylvania: Temple University Press.

Howell, J. and Elliott, J. R. (2018). Damages done: the longitudinal impacts of natural hazards on wealth inequality in the United States. *Social Problems*, 66(3), 448–467.

Hudson, B. M., Galloway, T. D., and Kaufman, J. L. (1979). Comparison of current planning theories: counterparts and contradictions. *Journal of the American Planning Association*, 45(4), 387–398.

Hung, W., Jonassen, D. H., and Liu, R. (2008). Problem-based learning. *Handbook of Research on Educational Communications and Technology*, 3(1), 485–506.

International Federation of Red Cross and Red Crescent Societies (IFRC). (2021). Disaster preparedness. Online. Available HTTP: ifrc.org/disaster-preparedness. Accessed 24 December, 2021.

International Federation of Red Cross and Red Crescent Societies (IFRC). (2021). National Society preparedness for effective response. Online. Available HTTP: https://oldmedia.ifrc. org/ifrc/what-we-do-disaster-and-crisis-national-society-preparedness-effective-response/. Accessed 3 January, 2022.

Israel, B. A., Coombe, C. M., Cheezum, R. R., Schulz, McGranaghan, R. J., Lichtenstein, R., Reyes, A. G., Clement, J., and Burris, A. (2010). Community-based participatory research: a capacity-building approach for policy advocacy aimed at eliminating health disparities. *American Journal of Public Health*, 100(11), 2094–2102.

Jackson, N. (2021). Personal interview, 13 May.

James, X., Hawkins, A., and Rowel, R. (2007). An assessment of the cultural appropriateness of emergency preparedness communication for low-income minorities. *Journal of Homeland Security and Emergency Management*, 4(3).

Jeans, H., Castillo, G.E., and Thomas, S., (2017). Absorb, Adapt, Transform: Resilience capacities. Oxfam. Online. Available HTTP: https://oxfamilibrary.openrepository.com/ bitstream/handle/10546/620178/gd-resilience-capacities-absorb-adapt-transform-250117- en.pdf?sequence=4. Accessed 24 December, 2021.

Jenkins, P. (2009). The nature of human communities. In D. S. K. Thomas, B. D. Phillips, W. E. Lovekamp and A. Fothergill (eds) Social Vulnerability to Disasters (2nd ed.). Boca Raton, Fl: CRC Press, p. 397

Jerolleman, A. (2021). Personal interview, 12 June.

Jerving, S., Jennings, K., Hirsch, M. M. and Rust, S. (2015). What Exxon knew about the earth's melting Arctic," *Los Angeles Times*, 9 October.

Johnson, Jamila (2021). Personal interview, 7 July.

Jones, L., Ludi, E., and Levine, S. (2010). Towards a characterisation of adaptive capacity: a framework for analysing adaptive capacity at the local level. Overseas Development Institute. Online. Available HTTP: https://oxfamilibrary.openrepository.com/bitstream/handle/10546/ 595168/bn-local-adaptive-capacity-011210.en.pdf?sequence=1. Accessed 24 December, 2021.

Joseph, S., Williams, R., and Yule, W. (1993). Changes in outlook following disaster: the preliminary development of a measure to assess positive and negative responses. *Journal of Traumatic Stress*, 6(2), 271–279.

Kaplan, A. (2000). Capacity building: shifting the paradigms of practice. *Development in Practice*, 10(3–4), 517–526.

Kapucu, N. (2008). Culture of preparedness: household disaster preparedness. *Disaster Prevention and Management: An International Journal*. 17(4), 526–535.

Karancı, A. N., & Akşit, B. (2000). Building disaster-resistant communities: Lessons learned from past earthquakes in Turkey and suggestions for the future. *International Journal of Mass Emergencies and Disasters*, 18(3), 403–416.

Karanci, A. N., Aksit, B., and Dirik, G. (2005). Impact of a community disaster awareness training program in Turkey: does it influence hazard-related cognitions and preparedness behaviors. *Social Behavior And Personality: An International Journal*, 33(3), 243–258.

Kelly, J. (2019). The Top 10 Causes of Global Warming. *Sciencing*. Online. Available HTTP: https://sciencing.com/the-top-10-causes-of-global-warming-12512484.html. Accessed 24 December, 2021.

Kelman, I., Mercer, J., and Gaillard, J. C. (2012). Indigenous knowledge and disaster risk reduction. *Geography*, 97(1), 12–21.

Khalid, A., and Azeem, M. (2012). Constructivist vs traditional: effective instructional approach in teacher education. *International Journal of Humanities and Social Science*, 2(5), 170–177.

Kim, H., and Zakour, M. (2017). Disaster preparedness among older adults: social support, community participation, and demographic characteristics. *Journal of Social Service Research*, 43(4), 498–509.

Kim, J. S. (2005). The effects of a constructivist teaching approach on student academic achievement, self-concept, and learning strategies. *Asia Pacific Education Review*, 6(1), 7–19.

King, D. W., Duello, T. M., Miranda, P. Y., Hodges, K. P., Shelton, A. J., Chukelu, P., and Jones, L. A. (2010). Strategies for recruitment of healthy pre-menopausal women into the African American Nutrition for Life (A NULIFE) study. *Journal of Women's Health*, 19(5), 855–862.

Kirkpatrick, J. D., and Kirkpatrick, W. K. (2016). Kirkpatrick's four levels of training evaluation. Association for Talent Development. Forthcoming.

Kitcher, P. (1980). A priori knowledge. *The Philosophical Review*, 89(1), 3–23.

Kousky, C., Ritchie, L., Tierney, K., and Lingle, B. (2019). Return on investment analysis and its applicability to community disaster preparedness activities: calculating costs and returns. *International Journal of Disaster Risk Reduction*, 41, 101296.

Krathwohl, D. R. (2002). A revision of Bloom's taxonomy: An overview. *Theory Into Practice*, 41(4), 212–218.

Lachlan, K. A., Burke, J., Spence, P. R., and Griffin, D. (2009). Risk perceptions, race, and Hurricane Katrina. *The Howard Journal of Communications*, 20(3), 295–309.

Laerd Statistics (n.d.). Friedman Test in SPSS. Online. Available HTTP: https://statistics.laerd.com/spss-tutorials/friedman-test-using-spss-statistics.php. Accessed 24 December, 2021.

Lambert, L. (2013). Trading rights for greenhouse gases: the dilemma of cap-and-trade and environmental justice. *George Mason University Civil Rights Law Journal*, 24, 205.

Laska, S., and Morrow, B. H. (2006). Social vulnerabilities and Hurricane Katrina: an unnatural disaster in New Orleans. *Marine Technology Society Journal*, 40(4), 16–26.

Lavigne, S. (2021). Personal interview, 11 April.

Levac, J., Toal-Sullivan, D., and O'Sullivan, T. L. (2012). Household emergency preparedness: a literature review. *Journal of Community Health*, 37(3), 725–733.

Levin, L. S. (1992). Listen to the community. *World Health 1992*, May–June: 10–11.

Levine, S., Ludi, E., and Jones, L. (2011) Rethinking Support for Adaptive Capacity to Climate Change, ODI. Online. Available HTTP: http://www.fsnnetwork.org/sites/default/files/accra_rethinking_support_report_final_levine_ludi_jones_2011.pdf. Accessed 24 December, 2021.

Leviton, L. C. (2003). Commentary: engaging the community in evaluation: bumpy, time consuming, and important. *American Journal of Evaluation*, 24(1), 85–90.

Liming, S. (2021). Getting to know the community: using Raymond Williams's concept of "knowable communities" to teach Wharton's Summer. In F. Asya (ed.) Teaching Edith Wharton's Major Novels and Short Fiction. London: Palgrave Macmillan, pp. 31–43.

Lindell, M. (2013). North American cities at risk: household responses to environmental hazards. In H. Joffe, T. Rossetto and J. Adams (eds) Cities at Risk. Dordrecht: Springer, pp. 109–130.

Lindell, M. K. (2013). Disaster studies. *Current Sociology*, 61(5–6), 797–825.

Lindholm, J., Carlson, T., Djupsund, G., Högväg, J., and Strandberg, K. (2015). Citizens' emotional and cognitive responses to focusing events: an experimental study. *International Journal of Mass Emergencies and Disasters*, 33(3), 1–5.

Lippmann, A. L. (2011). Disaster preparedness in vulnerable communities. *International Law and Policy Review*, 1(1), 69.

Logan, J. R. and Molotch, H. L. (1987). Urban Fortunes: The Political Economy of Place. Berkeley: University of California Press.

Look, D. W., and Spennemann, D. H. (2001). Disaster preparedness, planning, and mitigation. *CRM-WASHINGTON*, 24(8), 3–4.

Lovejoy, K., and Saxton, G. D. (2012). Information, community, and action: how nonprofit organizations use social media. *Journal of Computer-Mediated Communication*, 17(3), 337–353.

Macias, A. (2017). Teacher-led professional development: a proposal for a bottom-up structure approach. *International Journal of Teacher Leadership*, 8(1), 76–91.

Makondo, C. C., and Thomas, D. S. (2018). Climate change adaptation: linking indigenous knowledge with western science for effective adaptation. *Environmental Science and Policy*, 88, 83–91.

Mannan, M. S., and Kilpatrick, D. L. (2000). The pros and cons of shelter-in-place. *Process Safety Progress*, 19(4), 210–218.

Mäntysalo, R. (2005). Approaches to Participation in Urban Planning Theories. Rehabilitation of Suburban Areas. Online. Available HTTP: https://citeseerx.ist.psu.edu/viewdoc/download?doi=10.1.1.126.3107&rep=rep1&type=pdf. Accessed 24 December, 2021.

Marks, N., Abdallah, S., Simma, A. and Thompson, S. (2006). The Unhappy Planet Index, New Economics Foundation: London. Online. Available HTTP: http://www.neweconomics.org/.

Masterson, J. H., Peacock, W. G., Van Zandt, S. S., Grover, H., Schwarz, L. F., and Cooper, J. T. (2015). Planning for Community Resilience: A Handbook for Reducing Vulnerability to Disasters. Island Press/Center for Resource Economics. Washington, D.C.: Island Press.

Mazza, L. (2002). Technical knowledge and planning actions. *Planning Theory*, 1(1), 11–26.

McCoy, B., and Dash, N. (2013). Class. In D. S. K. Thomas, B. D. Phillips, W. E. Lovekamp and A. Fothergill (eds) Social Vulnerability to Disasters (2nd ed.). Boca Raton, Fl: CRC Press, pp. 83–112.

McEntire, D. A. (2015). Disaster Response and Recovery: Strategies and Tactics for Resilience. London: John Wiley and Sons.

Mercer, J., Kelman, I., Taranis, L., and Suchet-Pearson, S. (2010). Framework for integrating indigenous and scientific knowledge for disaster risk reduction. *Disasters*, 34(1), 214–239.

Mercer, N., Littleton, K., and Wegerif, R. (2009). Methods for studying the processes of interaction and collaborative activity in computer-based educational activities. In K. Kumpulainen, C. E. Hmelo-Silver and M. César (eds) Investigating Classroom Interaction. Rotterdam: Sense Publishers, pp. 27–42.

Molotch, H. (1976). The city as a growth machine: Toward a political economy of place. *American Journal of Sociology*, 82(2), 309–332.

Moore, Q. (2021). Personal interview, 23 April.

Moore, S., Daniel, M., Linnan, L., Campbell, M., Benedict, S., and Meier, A. (2004). After Hurricane Floyd passed: investigating the social determinants of disaster preparedness and recovery. *Family and Community Health*, 27(3), 204–217.

Morrow, B. H. (1999). Identifying and mapping community vulnerability. *Disasters*, 23(1), 1–18.

Motoyoshi, T. (2006). Public perception of flood risk and community-based disaster preparedness. In S. Ikeda, T. Fukuzono, and A. Sato (eds) Better Integrated Management of Disaster Risks: Toward Resilient Society to Emerging Disaster Risks in Mega-Cities. Tsukuba, Japan: National Research Institute for Earth Science and Disaster Prevention, 121–134.

MPH@GW. (2021). Equity vs. equality: What's the difference? The George Washington University Online Master of Public Health Program. Online. Available HTTP: https://onlinepublichealth.gwu.edu/resources/equity-vs-equality/. Accessed 24 December, 2021.

Murray, B. (2021). Personal interview, 15 March.

Musso, J. A., Kitsuse, A., and Cooper, T. L. (2002). Faith organizations and neighborhood councils in Los Angeles. *Public Administration and Development: The International Journal of Management Research and Practice*, 22(1), 83–94.

Mutch, C. (2014). The role of schools in disaster preparedness, response and recovery: what can we learn from the literature? *Pastoral Care in Education*, 32(1), 5–22.

Muttarak, R., and Lutz, W. (2014). Is education a key to reducing vulnerability to natural disasters and hence unavoidable climate change? *Ecology and Society*, 19(1).

Nakagawa, Y., and Shaw, R. (2004). Social capital: a missing link to disaster recovery. *International Journal of Mass Emergencies and Disasters*, 22(1), 5–34.

Nance, E. (2004). Putting participation in context: an evaluation of urban sanitation in Brazil. Stanford University.

Nance, E. (2009). Making the case for community-based laboratories: a new strategy for environmental justice. In R. D. Bullard and B. Wright (eds) Race, Place, and Environmental Justice after Hurricane Katrina: Struggles to Reclaim, Rebuild, and Revitalize New Orleans and the Gulf Coast. New York: Routledge, 154–155.

Nance, E. (2009). Responding to risk: the making of hazard mitigation strategy in post-Katrina New Orleans. *Journal of Contemporary Water Research and Education*, 141, 21–30.

Nance, E. (2010). Reforming mitigation programs: a New Orleans case analysis. *The Public Manager*, 39(3), 32–37.

Nance, E. (2012). Engineers and Communities: Transforming Sanitation in Contemporary Brazil, Lanham, MD: Lexington Books.

Nance, E. (2021). Comments to FEMA, in Maddie Sloan and Chrishelle Palay, Texas Appleseed-HOME FEMA RFI Comments, 21 July, 2021 (submitted to Robert J. Fenton, Federal Emergency Management Office).

Nance, E., and Ortolano, L. (2007). Community participation in urban sanitation: experiences in northeastern Brazil. *Journal of Planning Education and Research*, 26(3), 284–300.

NASA Global Climate Change. (2021a). Global Temperature. Online. Available HTTP: https://climate.nasa.gov/vital-signs/global-temperature/. Accessed 24 December, 2021.

NASA Global Climate Change. (2021b). Climate Change: How Do We Know? Online. Available HTTP: https://climate.nasa.gov/evidence/.

National Center for Disaster Preparedness. (2020). Preparedness attitudes and behaviors. National Center for Disaster Preparedness. Online. Available HTTP: https://ncdp.columbia.edu/research/preparedness-attitudes-behaviors/.

National Environmental Health Association (NEHA). (2021). Man-made hazard preparedness. Online. Available HTTP: https://www.neha.org/eh-topics/preparedness-0/man-made-hazard-preparedness. Accessed 3 January, 2022.

Nelson, B. (2021). Personal interview, 8 May.

NOAA. (2021). Climate Change: Global Sea Level. Online. Available HTTP: https://www.climate.gov/news-features/understanding-climate/climate-change-global-sea-level.

NOAA Global Monitoring Laboratory. (2021). Trends in Atmospheric Carbon Dioxide. Online. Available HTTP: https://gml.noaa.gov/ccgg/trends/.

NOAA National Centers for Environmental Information. (2021). U.S. Billion-Dollar Weather and Climate Disasters. Online. Available HTTPP: https://www.ncdc.noaa.gov/billions/. Accessed 24 December, 2021.

NOAA National Severe Storms Laboratory. (2013). Tornado basics: Severe Weather 101. Online. Available HTTP: https://www.nssl.noaa.gov/education/svrwx101/tornadoes/. Accessed 3 January, 2022.

NRDC. (2017). Climate Change and Health: Air Quality FAQS. Online. Available HTTP: https://www.nrdc.org/resources/climate-change-and-health-air-quality-faqs. Accessed 24 December, 2021.

Olsson, P., and Folke, C. (2001). Local ecological knowledge and institutional dynamics for ecosystem management: a study of Lake Racken watershed, Sweden. *Ecosystems*, 4(2), 85–104.

O'Reilly, E. D. and Snyde, A. (2021). Where Climate Change Will Hit the US Hardest, AXIOS. Online. Available HTTP: https://www.axios.com/where-climate-change-will-hit-the-us-hardest-1513303282-6566eea4-6369-4588-88cc-c2886db20b70.html Accessed 24 December, 2021.

Ostrom, T. M. (1969). The relationship between the affective, behavioral, and cognitive components of attitude. *Journal of Experimental Social Psychology*, 5(1), 12–30.

Oxford English Dictionary. (1989) Knowledge. In J. A. Simpson, and E. S. C. Weiner (eds), *Oxford English Dictionary*. Oxford: Oxford University Press.

Padgett, David (2021, 23 June). Personal interview.

Pandey, B. H., and Okazaki, K. (2005). Community-based disaster management: empowering communities to cope with disaster risks. *Regional Development Dialogue*, 26(2), 52.

Paris, D., and Alim, H. S. (eds) (2017). Culturally Sustaining Pedagogies: Teaching and Learning For Justice in a Changing World. New York: Teachers College Press.

Park, S., Mosley, J. E., and Grogan, C. M. (2018). Do residents of low-income communities' trust organizations to speak on their behalf? Differences by organizational type. *Urban Affairs Review*, 54(1), 137–164.

Pastor, M., Bullard, R., Boyce, J. K., Forthergill, A., MorelloFrosch, R., and Wright, B. (2006). In The Wake Of The Storm: Environment, Disaster, And Race After Katrina. New York: Russell Sage Foundation.

Paton, D. (2003). Disaster preparedness: a social-cognitive perspective. *Disaster Prevention and Management*, 12(3), 210–216.

Paton, D., and Johnston, D. (2001). Disasters and communities: vulnerability, resilience and preparedness. *Disaster Prevention and Management*, 10(4), 270–277.

Patton, M. Q. (1987). How To Use Qualitative Methods In Evaluation (No. 4). London: Sage.

Peacock, W. G., Gladwin, H., and Morrow, B. H. (1997). Hurricane Andrew: Ethnicity, Gender and the Sociology of Disasters. London: Routledge.

Pearce, D. (2003). Conceptual Framework for Analyzing the Distributive Impacts of Environmental Policies. OECD Environment Directorate. Online. Available HTTP: https://www.ucl.ac.uk/~uctpa36/oecd%20distribution.pdf. Accessed 6 January, 2022.

Peek, L. (2013). Age. In D. S. K. Thomas, B. D. Phillips, W. E. Lovekamp and A. Fothergill (eds) Social Vulnerability to Disasters (2nd ed.). Boca Raton, Fl: CRC Press, pp. 167–198.

Peek, L., Tobin, J., Adams, R. M., Wu, H., & Mathews, M. C. (2020). A framework for convergence research in the hazards and disaster field: The Natural Hazards Engineering Research Infrastructure CONVERGE facility. *Frontiers in Built Environment*, 6, 110.

Peek, L. (2021). Personal interview, 12 June.

Pelling M., Obrien, K., and Matyas, D. (2014) Adaptation and transformation. *Climate Change*, 133(1), 113–127.

Perkins, D. D., and Zimmerman, M. A. (1995). Empowerment theory, research, and application. *American Journal of Community Psychology*, 23(5), 569–579.

Perry, R. W. (1987). Disaster preparedness and response among minority citizens, In: R. R. Dynes et al. (eds), Sociology of Disaster: Contribution of Sociology to Disaster Research, Milan, Italy: Franco Angeli, pp. 135–152.

Perry, R. W. (2007). What is a disaster? In Handbook of Disaster Research. New York: Springer, p. 9.

Peyronnin, N., Green, M., Richards, C. P., Owens, A., Reed, D., Chamberlain, J., ... and Belhadjali, K. (2013). Louisiana's 2012 Coastal Master Plan: overview of a science-based and publicly informed decision-making process. *Journal of Coastal Research*, 67(10067), 1–15.

Pipa, T. (2006). In disaster planning, focus on local charities. *The Chronicle of Philanthropy*, 29.

Popple, K., and Quinney, A. (2002). Theory and practice of community development: a case study from the United Kingdom. *Community Development*, 33(1), 71–85.

Pranis, K. (2001). Restorative justice, social justice, and the empowerment of marginalized populations. In Bazemore, G. and Mara Schiff (eds). Restorative Community Justice: Repairing Harm and Transforming Communities. Nantucket, MA: Anderson Publishing, pp. 287–306.

Preece, J. (2004). Etiquette, empathy and trust in communities of practice: stepping-stones to social capital. *Journal of University Computer Science*, 10(3), 294–302.

Prezenski, S., Brechmann, A., Wolff, S., and Russwinkel, N. (2017). A cognitive modeling approach to strategy formation in dynamic decision making. *Frontiers in Psychology*, 8, 1335.

Purdy, L. (2011). Project proposal for the Manchester Food Co-op: bringing the community to the table. Doctoral dissertation, Southern New Hampshire University.

Raju, S. S. (2017). Understanding community: baseline surveys. In S. Raju (ed.) Corporate Social Responsibility in India. Singapore: Springer, pp. 99–131.

Ramasubramanian, L. (2015). Engaging vulnerable populatons using participatory mapping: lessons learned and guidelines for community advocates and transportaton planners. *Journal of the Urban and Regional Information Systems Associaton*, 26(2), 25–32.

Reed, S. (2021) His family ravaged by cancer, an angry Louisiana man wages war on the very air that he breathes. *People*, 35(11). Online. Available HTTP: http://www.people.com/people/archive/0,,20114739,00.html. Accessed 6 June 2016.

Rice University. (2018). Natural disasters widen racial wealth gap: study also finds FEMA aid increased inequality. *ScienceDaily*. Online. Available HTTP: https://www.sciencedaily.com/releases/2018/08/180820164234.htm. Accessed 6 June 2016.

Ricketts, K. G. (2016). Community power: bringing the right people to the table. *Community and Economic Development Publications*. 11. Online. Available HTTP: https://uknowledge.uky.edu/ced_reports/11. Accessed 6 June 2016.

Rigling, L. and Cross, W. (2019). Getting to know you: how we turned community knowledge into open advocacy. In A. Wesolek, J. Lashley and A. Langley (eds) OER: A Field Guide for Academic Librarians. Oregon: Pacific University Press, pp. 193–212.

Rini, D. S., and Adisyahputra, D. V. S. (2020). Boosting student critical thinking ability through project-based learning, motivation, and visual, auditory, kinesthetic learning style. *Universal Journal of Educational Research*, 8(4), 37–44.

Risky Business (2014). The Economic Risks of Climate Change in the United States. Online. Available HTTP: https://riskybusiness.org/site/assets/uploads/2015/09/RiskyBusiness_Report_WEB_09_08_14.pdf. Accessed 2 January, 2022.

Ross, A. (1986). Why do we believe what we are told? *Ratio* 1, 69–88. Online. Available HTTP: https://philpapers.org/archive/ROSWDW-3.pdf. Accessed 6 June 2016.

Runyan, R. C. (2006). Small business in the face of crisis: identifying barriers to recovery from a natural disaster 1. *Journal of Contingencies and Crisis Management*, 14(1), 12–26.

Russell, B. (2020). A priori justification and knowledge, in N. Zalta (ed.) The Stanford Encyclopedia of Philosophy. Online. Available HTTP: https://plato.stanford.edu/archives/sum2020/entries/apriori/.

Saegert, S., Thompson, J. P., and Warren, M. R. (eds). (2002). Social Capital and Poor Communities. New York: Russell Sage Foundation.

Savery, J. R. (2015). Overview of problem-based learning: definitions and distinctions. *Essential Readings in Problem-Based Learning: Exploring and Extending The Legacy of Howard S. Barrows*, 9(2), 5–15.

Scandlyn, J., Thomas, S. K., and Brett, J. (2013). Theoretical framing of worldviews, values, and structural dimensions. In D. S. K. Thomas, B. D. Phillips, W. E. Lovekamp, and A. Fothergill. Social Vulnerability to Disasters (2nd ed.). Boca Raton, Fl: CRC Press, pp. 33–56.

Schmidtlein, M. C., Deutsch, R. C., Piegorsch, W. W., and Cutter, S. L. (2008). A sensitivity analysis of the social vulnerability index. *Risk Analysis: An International Journal*, 28(4), 1099–1114.

Schoch-Spana, M., Gill, K., Hosangadi, D., Slemp, C., Burhans, R., Zeis, J., and Links, J. (2019). Top-down and bottom-up measurement to enhance community resilience to disasters. *American Journal of Public Health*, 109(S4), S265–S267.

Schultz, C. H., Koenig, K. L., and Noji, E. K. (2002). Disaster preparedness. Emergency Medicine Concepts and Clinical Practice. St. Louis: Mosby, 2631-0.

Schwab, J., Topping, K. C., Eadie, C. C., Deyle, R. E., and Smith, R. A. (1998). Planning for post-disaster recovery and reconstruction. Chicago, IL: American Planning Association, pp. 483–484.

Scott, D. E., and Scott, S. (2016). Leadership for quality university teaching: how bottom-up academic insights can inform top-down leadership. *Educational Management Administration and Leadership*, 44(3), 511–531.

Scripps Institution of Oceanography. (2019). Carbon Dioxide Levels Hit Record Peak in May. University of California-San Diego. Online. Available HTTP: https://scripps.ucsd.edu/news/carbon-dioxide-levels-hit-record-peak-may.

Semien, J., and Nance, E. (2019). KAPS: a disaster training approach for high-risk communities. *International Journal of Mass Emergencies and Disasters*, 37(3). P 264–285

Shah Alam Khan, M. (2008), Disaster preparedness for sustainable development in Bangladesh, *Disaster Prevention and Management*, 17(5), 662–671.

Shelton, K. and Nance, E. (2019). Development Regulations. Greater Houston Flood Mitigation Consortium. Online. Available HTTP: https://www.houstonconsortium.com.

Stanford Report (2006). Science study predicts collapse of all seafood fisheries by 2050. Online. Available HTTP: https://news.stanford.edu/news/2006/november8/ocean-110806.html.

Steinfeld, H., Gerber, P., Wassenaar, T., Castel, V., Rosales, M., and De Haan, C. (2006). Livestock's long shadow. Food and Agriculture Organisation of the United Nations (FAO). Available HTTP: https://www.fao.org/publications/card/en/c/9655af93-7f88-58fc-84e8-d70a9a4d8bec/. Accessed 6 June 2021.

Stephens, N. (2021). Personal interview, 5 June.

Stone, K. V. W. (1980). The post-war paradigm in American labor law. *Yale Law Journal*, 90, 1509.

Stop Formosa Plastics. (n.d.). Stop Formosa Plastics Protect Our Community. Online. Available HTTP: https://www.stopformosa.org/.

Substance Abuse and Mental Health Services Administration (SAMHSA). (2014). Improving cultural competence. Treatment Improvement Protocol (TIP) Series No. 59. HHS Publication No. (SMA) 14-4849. Rockville, MD: Substance Abuse and Mental Health Services Administration.

Suda, C. A. (2000). Natural disaster preparedness, environmental degradation and sustainable development in Kenya. *African Study Monographs*, 21(3), 91–103.

Sutton, J., and Tierney, K. (2006). Disaster Preparedness: Concepts, Guidance, and Research. Colorado: University of Colorado, 3, 1–41.

Swanson, L. A. (2013). A strategic engagement framework for nonprofits. *Nonprofit Management and Leadership*, 23(3), 303–323.

Sweet, W. V., Kopp, R. E., Weaver, C. P., Obeysekera, J., Horton, R. M., Thieler, E. R., and Zervas, C. (2017). Global and Regional Sea Level Rise Scenarios for the United States. NOAA Technical Report NOS CO-OPS 083 (January 2017). National Oceanic and Atmospheric Administration, Silver Spring, MD.

Takahashi, R., Anderson, R. D., Coover, S., Kikuch, K., Scott, A. D., and Smith, R. R. (2014). The FEMA and CERT: Training, guidance and managements, an analysis on cross-cultural perspectives. *Odisha Journal of Social Science*, 1, 14–28.

Takvorian, F., Forbis, P., Holmquist, S., LoPresti, T., and Benson, L. (2012). Community planning for power. In G. Johnson, S. A. Rainey-Brown, and R. D. S. Gragg (eds) Environmental Justice Reader, II. Ronkonkoma: Linus Publications, pp. 423–425.

TANGO International. (2018). Methodological Guide: A Guide for Calculating Resilience Capacity. Produced by TANGO International as part of the Resilience Evaluation, Analysis and Learning (REAL) Associate Award.

Terpstra, T. (2011). Emotions, trust, and perceived risk: affective and cognitive routes to flood preparedness behavior. *Risk Analysis: An International Journal*, 31(10), 1658–1675.

Tewdwr-Jones, M. (1998). Rural government and community participation: the planning role of community councils. *Journal of Rural Studies*, 14(1), 51–62.

Thomas, D. S. K., Hyde I., and Meyer, M. (2009). Measuring and Conveying Social Vulnerability to Disasters. Boca Raton, Fl: CRC Press.

Thomas, D. S., Phillips, B. D., Fothergill, A., and Blinn-Pike, L. (2009). Social Vulnerability to Disasters. Boca Raton, Fl: CRC Press.

Thomas, T. N., Leander-Griffith, M., Harp, V., and Cioffi, J. P. (2015). Influences of preparedness knowledge and beliefs on household disaster preparedness. *Morbidity and Mortality Weekly Report*, 64(35), 965–971.

Thompson, A. (2020). A running list of record-breaking natural disasters in 2020. *Scientific American*, December 22. Online. Available HTTP: https://www.scientificamerican.com/article/a-running-list-of-record-breaking-natural-disasters-in-2020/.

Tierney, K. J. (1997). Business impacts of the Northridge earthquake. *Journal of Contingencies and Crisis Management*, 5(2), 87–97.

Tierney, K. (2014). The Social Roots of Risk: Producing Disaster, Promoting Resilience. Stanford: Stanford Business Books.

Tilman, D., Balzer, C., Hill, J., and Befort, B. L. (2011). Global food demand and the sustainable intensification of agriculture. *Proceedings of the National Academy of Sciences*, 108(50), 20260–20264.

Tobias, C. R., Downes, A., Eddens, S., and Ruiz, J. (2012). Building blocks for peer success: lessons learned from a train-the-trainer program. *AIDS patient care and STDs*, 26(1), 53–59.

Tobin-Gurley, J. and Enarson, E. (2013). Gender. In D. S. K. Thomas, B. D. Phillips, W. E. Lovekamp, and A. Fothergill (eds) Social Vulnerability to Disasters (2nd ed.). Boca Raton, FL: CRC Press, pp. 139–165.

Trenberth, K. E. (2018). Climate change caused by human activities is happening and it already has major consequences. *Journal of Energy & Natural Resources Law*, 36(4), 463–481.

Tweed, F., and Walker, G. (2011). Some lessons for resilience from the 2011 multi-disaster in Japan. *Local Environment*, 16(9), 937–942.

UNHCR. (2008). Designing Participatory Workshops. United Nations High Commissioner for Refugees: 1–172. EPDF Files. UNHCR ECentre in Collaboration with InterWorks, LL, Jan. 2008. Available HTTP: http://epdfiles.engr.wisc.edu/dmcweb/EP05DesigningParticipatory Workshops.pdf. Accessed 21 July, 2016.

United Nations. (2017). World population projected to reach 9.8 billion in 2050, and 11.2 billion in 2100. Online. Available HTTP: https://www.un.org/development/desa/en/news/population/world-population-prospects-2017.html.

United Nations. 2021. United Nations Framework Convention on Climate Change. https://unfccc.int https://unfccc.int/resource/docs/convkp/conveng.pdf

United States Environmental Protection Agency (U.S. EPA). (2021). TRI Explorer 2019 Updated Dataset [Internet database]. Online. Available HTTP: https://enviro.epa.gov/triexplorer/. Accessed 29 August, 2021.

US Census Bureau. (2010). Population Estimates, February, 2016 (V2017)—Geismar, LA [data table]. Quick Facts. Online. Available HTTP: https://www.census.gov/quickfacts/fact/table/Geismar/. Accessed 16 February 2016.

US Department of Commerce, N. O. and A. A. (2013). What is a Tornado? NOAA's National Ocean Service. Online. Available HTTP: https://oceanservice.noaa.gov/facts/tornado.html.

US Global Change Research Program. (2016). The Impacts of Climate Change on Human Health in the United States: A Scientific Assessment. A. Crimmins, J. Balbus, J. L. Gamble, C. B. Beard, J. E. Bell, D. Dodgen, R. J. Eisen, N. Fann, M. D. Hawkins, S. C. Herring, L. Jantarasami, D. M. Mills, S. Saha, M. C. Sarofim, J. Trtanj, and L. Ziska, (eds). Washington, DC: U.S. Global Change Research Program.

Van Zandt S., Peacock, W.G., Henry, D. W., Grover, H., Highfield, W. E., and Brody, S. D. (2012). Mapping social vulnerability to enhance housing and neighborhood resilience. *Housing Policy Debate*, 22(1), 29–55,

The VARK modalities. (n.d.). Introduction to the Vark Modalities. Online. Available HTTP: https://vark-learn.com/introduction-to-vark/the-vark-modalities/. Retrieved on 1 July, 2019, from vark-learn.com/introduction-to-vark/the-vark-modalities/.

Vaughan, E. (2018). Resilience Measurement Practical Guidance Note Series 3: Resilience Capacity Measurement. Produced by Mercy Corps as part of the Resilience Evaluation, Analysis and Learning (REAL) Associate Award. Online. Available HTTP: https://resiliencelinks.org/system/files/download-count/documents/2019-08/gn03_resilience_capacity_measurement_final508_0.pdf. Accessed 19 March 2020.

Vaughan, M. B. (2020) Kaiāulu: Gathering Tides. Corvallis, Oregon: Oregon State University Press.

Von Glasersfeld, E. (1974). Piaget and the radical constructivist epistemology. In C. D. Smock, and E. von Glasersfeld (eds). Epistemology and Education. Athens, GA: Follow Through Publications, pp. 1–24.

Von Glasersfeld, E. (1989). Constructivism in education. In T. Husen, and T. N. Postlethwaite (eds) The International Encyclopedia of Education Research and Studies. Oxford/New York: Pergamon Press, pp. 162–163.

Von Glasersfeld, E. (1994). A radical constructivist view of basic mathematical concepts. In P. Ernest (ed.) Constructing Mathematical Knowledge: Epistemology and Mathematics Education. London: Falmer Press, pp. 5–7.

Wade, D., Crompton, D., Howard, A., Stevens, N., Metcalf, O., Brymer, M.,... and Forbes, D. (2014). Skills for psychological recovery: evaluation of a post-disaster mental health training program. *Disaster Health*, 2(3–4), 138–145.

Walker, G., and Burningham, K. (2011). Flood risk, vulnerability and environmental justice: Evidence and evaluation of inequality in a UK context. *Critical Social Policy*, 31(2), 216–240.

Wallace, R. A., and Wolf, A. (2006). Contemporary Sociological Theory: Expanding the Classical Tradition (6th ed.). Upper Saddle River, NJ: Prentice-Hall.

Wang, G. G., and Wilcox, D. (2006). Training evaluation: knowing more than is practiced. *Advances in Developing Human Resources*, 8(4), 528–539.

Warburton, J., and McLaughlin, D. (2007). Passing on our culture: how older Australians from diverse cultural backgrounds contribute to civil society. *Journal of Cross-cultural Gerontology*, 22(1), 47–60.

Webb, S. (2009). Investing human capital and healthy rebuilding in the aftermath of Hurricane Katrina. In R. Bullard (ed.). Race, Place, and Environmental Justice After Hurricane Katrina. Boulder, CO: Westview Press, pp. 229–248.

Weber, E. U., and Hsee, C. (1998). Cross-cultural differences in risk perception, but cross-cultural similarities in attitudes towards perceived risk. *Management Science*, 44(9), 1205–1217.

Wells, C. (2013). Disasters: the role of institutional responses in shaping public perceptions of death. In R. Lee and D. Morgan (eds) Death Rites. London: Routledge, pp. 213–238.

Whitehead, L., Warren, R. C., Johnson, G. S., and Francesca, L. M. (2012). Mississippi head start mothers: an environmental justice case study: the struggle for environmental justice in the Louisiana Chemical Corridor. In G. Johnson, S. A. Rainey-Brown, and R. D. S. Gragg (eds) Environmental Justice Reader II: A Survey and Review of Critical Issues in Disenfranchised and Vulnerable Communities in the Twenty-First Century. Ronkonkoma, N.Y.: Linus Publications, pp. 423–425.

Wijkman, A., and Timberlake, L. (1984). Natural Disasters. Acts of God or Acts of Man? London: Earthscan.

Williams, S. W. (2001). The effectiveness of subject matter experts as technical trainers. *Human Resource Development Quarterly*, 12(1), 91.

Wilson, S. M. (2009). An ecologic framework to study and address environmental justice and community health issues. *Environmental Justice*, 2(1), 15–24.

Wingate, M. S., Perry, E. C., Campbell, P. H., David, P., and Weist, E. M. (2007). Identifying and protecting vulnerable populations in public health emergencies: addressing gaps in education and training. *Public Health Reports*, 122(3), 422–426.

Winsemius, H. C., Jongman, B., Veldkamp, T. I., Hallegatte, S., Bangalore, M., and Ward, P. J. (2018). Disaster risk, climate change, and poverty: assessing the global exposure of poor people to floods and droughts. *Environment and Development Economics*, 23(3), 328–348.

Wisner B. (2004). Assessment of capability and vulnerability. In G. Bankoff, G. Frerks and D. Hilhorst (eds). Mapping Vulnerability: Disasters, Development, and People. London: Earthscan, pp. 183–193.

Wood, D. F. (2003). Problem based learning. *BMJ*, 326(7384), 328–330.

World Economic Forum. (2016). The New Plastics Economy: Rethinking the future of plastics. Online. Available HTTP: http://www3.weforum.org/docs/WEF_The_New_Plastics_Economy.pdf.

Worm, B., Barbier, E. B., Beaumont, N., Duffy, J. E., Folke, C., Halpern, B. S., Jackson, J. B., Lotze, H. K., Micheli, F., Palumbi, S. R. and Sala, E. (2006). Impacts of biodiversity loss on ocean ecosystem services. *Science*, 314(5800), 787–790.

Wright, B. (2009). Policy and Research. Deep South Center for Environmental Justice. Web. Online. Available HTTP: https://www.dscej.org/our-work/research-and-policy. Accessed 10 March 2016.

Wright, B. (2012). Endangered communities: the struggle for environmental justice in the Louisiana chemical corridor. In G. Johnson, S. A. Rainey-Brown, and R. D. S. Gragg. Environmental Justice Reader, II. Ronkonkoma, N.Y.: Linus Publications, pp. 423–425.

Wright, B., and Nance, E. (2012). Toward equity: Prioritizing vulnerable communities in climate change. *Duke Forum for Law and Social Change*, 4, 1.

Xiao, Y., and Van Zandt, S. (2012). Building community resiliency: Spatial links between household and business post-disaster return. *Urban Studies*, 49(11), 2523–2542.

Xiao, Y., Wu, K., Finn, D., and Chandrasekhar, D. Community businesses as social units in post-disaster recovery. *Journal of Planning Education and Research*. October 2018. 10.11 77/0739456X18804328

Yale. (n.d.) Shelter in place. Shelter in Place Emergency Management. Online. Available HTTP: https://emergency.yale.edu/be-prepared/shelter-place.

Yang, T., and Warburton, D. E. (2018). Indigenous elders' role in fostering intergenerational relationships with youth. *The Health and Fitness Journal of Canada*, 11(4), 88–93.

Yates, F. (1934). Contingency tables. *Journal of the Royal Statistical Society*, 1, 217–235.

Yinger, J. (1991). Acts of discrimination: evidence from the 1989 housing discrimination study. *Journal of Housing Economics*, 1(4), 318–346.

Yli-Pelkonen, V., and Kohl, J. (2005). The role of local ecological knowledge in sustainable urban planning: perspectives from Finland. *Sustainability, Science, and Policy*, 1(1), 1–14.

Young, H. P. (1994). Equity: In Theory and Practice. Princeton, NJ: Princeton University Press.

Zajac, E. E. (1996). Political Economy of Fairness. Cambridge Massachusetts: MIT Press.

Zalasiewicz, J., Waters, C. N., Williams, M., and Summerhayes, C. P. (eds) (2019). The Anthropocene as a Geological Time Unit: A Guide to the Scientific Evidence and Current Debate. Cambridge: Cambridge University Press.

Zaman, S., Sammonds, P., Ahmed, B., and Rahman, T. (2020). Disaster risk reduction in conflict contexts: lessons learned from the lived experiences of Rohingya refugees in Cox's Bazar, Bangladesh. *International Journal of Disaster Risk Reduction*, 50, 101694.

Ziervogel, G., Cowen, A., and Ziniades, J. (2016). Moving from adaptive to transformative capacity: building foundations for inclusive, thriving, and regenerative urban settlements. *Sustainability*, 8(9), 955.

Zimmerman, M. A. (2000). Empowerment theory. In J. Rappaport, and E. Seidman (eds) Handbook of Community Psychology. Boston, MA: Springer, pp. 43–63.

Index

Page numbers in *italics* refer to figures, those in **bold** indicate boxes, *a* denotes appendices.